STRENGTH FOR THE ROAD

Mark Stevens

gbl Great Big Life
PUBLISHING

Published in 2014 by Great Big Life Publishing
Empower Centre, 83-87 Kingston Road, Portsmouth, PO2 7DX, UK

British Library Cataloguing in Publication Data.

A catalogue record for this book is available from the British Library.

ISBN-13: 978-0-9928027-6-9
EBOOK: 978-0-9928027-7-6

ENDORSEMENTS

'This book represents seventeen years of Mark's experience in the local church as a musician, singer, songwriter, actor, creative director and worship leader; but above all team player and servant in God's house. His heart for worship and unique ability to lead people into God's presence has been a consistent hallmark of Mark's life and ministry. Mark's insights, understanding and wisdom in the area of worship will help us all to go beyond what we've previously known, to new levels of encounter with God. I've known Mark for over fifteen years. He is a wonderful combination of generous, kind, caring, compassionate, crazy and hilarious. Mark is also my son-in-law; he's a great husband to our daughter Beth and fantastic father to Jonah and Sienna, two of our beautiful grandchildren.'

Pastor Paul Scanlon

'Mark's book is so compelling that I could not put it down! He tells his story of the fame of being a national childhood television star, only to fall into the trap of a horrific ten-year drug addiction. Much like the Apostle Paul, Mark had a face-to-face encounter with Christ that totally set him free and turned his life completely around. Today, Mark is one of the most anointed worship leaders I have ever encountered, but even more important is that he lives a life of worship every day. He has told his story in all of our Mercy homes around the world, as well as leading our staff and residents into the very presence of God. Mark would be a huge blessing to any church or ministry!'

Nancy Alcorn,
Founder and President of Mercy Ministries International

'Mark Stevens' book *Strength for the Road* captivated me. Mark shares deep and profound insights that thrilled my heart. I highly recommend it. It ushers you right into the immediate presence of God.'

Reinhard Bonnke,
Evangelist

'Mark is a gifted and spirit-led worship leader and pastor. Over the years, I have come to know Mark as both a friend and a co-labourer in the Kingdom. I have watched his heart and passion to connect people to Jesus and to see churches everywhere strong in the things of worship – he is an inspiring individual! This book is a tribute to the years of experience Mark has gained under godly leadership and the fruit of the Spirit at work in his own life. I know you will be blessed and gain fresh insight as you glean from the pages of this book.'

Reuben T. Morgan,
Hillsong Church

'Mark Stevens shouldn't be alive. After 'making it' in the world of entertainment his fall from dizzy heights is jaw dropping. This book is the inside story. It's the stuff of boy to man, lost to found. It tracks the restoration of mangled to miraculous and then hands out diamonds by the truck load formed from the intense heat of the journey. Mark is a miracle. These truths are not made up. This is both a lifesaver and life-giver to all who want to go beyond their past into their magnificent future. Mark, I salute you for all you've become.'

Dave Gilpin,
Senior Pastor, Hope City Church, England

Mark is a very easy person to work with. He has a depth of understanding and an experience of people that is reassuring and very helpful to leaders looking to develop their teams. This book is refreshing and challenging and also provokes us to examine the heart of worship within each of us as we make Him the centre of our lives. I wholly and enthusiastically would recommend this book to all leaders of churches. It is great to be working with Mark, who is not just a consultant but a practitioner of the highest calibre. This book, will I believe prove to be a valuable tool for the transformation of many churches as they aspire to worship God in authentic, prophetic worship.

Pastor Paul Hallam
Lead Pastor, The Lighthouse, UK

CONTENTS

FOREWORD

A great book can only be written by someone who has greatness within them. In my experience greatness is produced and becomes evident in people who have been through great struggles, developed great and godly character during these testing times, and have come out with experience in God which results in a real desire to share their deep experience, strength and hope with others.

Mark Stevens has been a close personal friend of mine for many years now, therefore I know him well. I can testify that he is a man of God. His family is godly and remarkable. He and his wife Beth have two lovely children, Jonah and Sienna.

Mark has learned through the highs and lows of his life that there is only one place to go for solace and breakthrough, and that is into the very presence of God Himself, into that deep place, the secret place of close and beautiful communion with God. I see in Mark a call to walk close to God. He has had to pay a price for this but when you meet with him you come away thinking, 'This man has been with God.' There is that special anointing about him that few carry.

Mark has learned, too, that to maintain a strong and victorious spiritual life we must learn to cry out to God during not only the bad times but through the good times also.

Mark's book will inspire you to go deeper with God. He shares the secrets of deep and true worship. Through his life he has learned to experience God, you will learn to do this too.

I have been with Mark as he has led thousands in worship or simply shared his testimony. He has been as humble when singing in a crusade with Evangelist Reinhard Bonnke or Darlene Zschech as he is when leading a group of homeless people into their first experience of the presence of God. These are qualities that not many have. This is why he is my friend. I consider it an honour to write this Foreword.

John Edwards
Walking Free Ministries

DEDICATION

To my beautiful wife Beth. You are my best friend, my confidant. I thank God everyday that I'm able to walk this road with you and next to you.

I love you.

The best is yet to come.

Hubby xx

ACKNOWLEDGEMENTS

There are quite a number of incredible people that I would like to acknowledge and say thank you to who have both inspired me and helped in the journey of writing this book.

Beth
My beautiful bride. I love you. Words could never express how much you mean to me. Thank you for your unwavering belief in me. And thank you for encouraging me to write this book. The best is definitely yet to come.

Paul and Glenda Scanlon
My wonderful in-laws. You are extraordinary people. I'm so thankful that I get to do life with you both. Thank you for your unwavering love and support. And thank you for your huge giving hearts.

John Edwards
You, my friend, are a miracle and an inspiration. You are also one of my best and dearest friends. While I was writing this book you were going through chemo therapy for Hep C, yet you still encouraged and supported me. You prayed for me and

sacrificially gave of your time to ensure this book was completed. You also helped this be a stronger book so that it could be strength to others. You never cease to amaze me with the strength you exude. No eye has seen, bro . . .

Dave Gilpin

Dave, you helped this be a better book. I don't think you realise how poignant our meeting together was. Thank you for investing some of your precious time into helping me dig deeper and say things the way I really wanted to say them – with more authenticity! And, thank you for helping release the danger in me!

Nigel Ipinson-Fleming

Nigel, you have been an incredible source of encouragement. On the odd day where I have felt small, just a conversation with you and I have felt like I can take on the world again. Thank you for your friendship.

Andy Elmes

Thank you for being the spark that caused this book to come to life! Your encouragement provoked me to begin the journey. This book has changed a lot along the way, however it still captures the essence of some of the original things we discussed before its conception.

Matt Lockwood

You, my friend, were also a great encouragement and great source of wisdom during this book's conception. Thank you for your encouragement and creativity.

Bob and Jane Baker

Thank you for your efforts in helping proof read my book. I appreciate it immensely!

LORD Jesus

It would take me a million life times to describe what You mean to me. You are my everything – the very breath in my lungs. You are the rock I stand upon. You saved me and rescued me from despair and put a new song in my mouth. I will love You for all of my days. You are the very reason why I wrote this book, to share with others the wonderful things You have done for me.

INTRODUCTION

The heart behind this book is to strengthen, encourage and equip you for the road ahead.

Life is an incredible journey, full of twists and turns, mountains and valleys, victories and challenges. The reality is we never really know what each day will hold for us. Much of life is a surprise. With each step we take we are presented with something that we may never have seen before. With each corner we turn there will be something different to embrace or confront. Life also has a momentum to it. A generation is born, it grows and then passes away as another generation steps forward. The earth keeps turning, the tide keeps changing and the waves continuously roll in. There is constant movement as life forges its own path.

However, in the midst of continuous change there is one thing that we can find stability and strength in: God's Word. The Bible says in Isaiah 40:8,

> *"The grass withers, the flower fades but the Word of our God stands forever."*

God's Word will stand throughout all generations. It is the one thing that will endure and will cause our lives to rise to new heights. His Word is a rock and a sure foundation that we can find refuge in when life overtakes us, overwhelms us or challenges us to our core. His Word is also a constant source of strength, hope, joy and encouragement.

In this book I wanted to open up my life to you and share some of the truths I have learned from God's Word which have helped me overcome. I believe they will enrich your life. There have been seasons in my life where the road I have taken is full of people who are on the same path. There have been numerous relationships to draw encouragement and strength from. Yet there have also been times where the road I have taken has been relationally scarce – just God and me. Friend, I have seen God's faithfulness on both roads so I know without a shadow of doubt that God's faithfulness will be evident to you on the road you are on as well.

At times I have failed to realise how much our lives can impact another person. But over time I have come to understand that our lives are wonderfully influential and incredibly compelling. My prayer for you as you read this book is that you will be impacted by these chapters and will find a source of courage and strength in them for they have been drawn from my own personal journey. I want you to understand that there is someone out there who has gone through what you're going through, a person who 'gets you'. My other prayer is that you would begin to realise just how powerful *your* personal story is! Friend, your life was meant to have a positive effect on somebody. Your life was designed to be the strength and fuel that somebody desperately needs in order to overcome. Your life counts for something, never doubt that!

Now, I have seen and experienced a lot of things in my forty-something years on the planet and, to tell you the truth, I shouldn't have lived through some of them. But by the grace of God I am still here. I made it out alive! This book is a collection of experiences that I have specifically chosen because of the truth they carry, which has helped keep me sane and press on through! Some of the chapters are based on my own personal testimony and my experience in church leadership, while others are based on biblical characters that have radically impacted my life. Some talk about the richness of God's presence, others about the real worshipper within us all, and yet others talk about overcoming trials of the soul. They have been strength for the road I have taken. I pray that as you read them they would be *STRENGTH FOR YOUR ROAD* too!

Enjoy!

Mark

CHAPTER 1

DEAR DEVIL, YOU SHOULD HAVE KILLED ME WHILE YOU HAD THE CHANCE!

"They overcame him [the devil] by the blood of the Lamb and by the word of their testimony, and they did not love their lives to the death."

Revelation 12:11

The day before I encountered Jesus Christ I had been invited to a party at my ex-girlfriend's house. I now understand that it was a divine set-up.

I arrived four hours late, along with my drug dealer and a friend of his. As you can imagine we were reluctantly invited in. Straight after walking through the door my drug dealer and his friend went into the bathroom to shoot up heroin. They forgot to lock the door and were walked in on. I was in the lounge trying to get everyone pumped up to party some more but they weren't having any of it. I heard a commotion break out in the hallway. There was lots of shouting and a real carry on happening as my ex-girlfriend's neighbour proceeded to kick out my friends! All of a sudden my ex-girlfriend walked towards me, swiftly collared me, dragged me into her bedroom and then pushed me up against the wall. She strongly said to me, 'Mark Stevens, enough is enough! What are you doing inviting those guys to my house! And what on earth are you doing with your life? You're destroying yourself!'

I remember sliding down the wall, cupping my head in my hands saying these words:

'I don't know. I have no idea what I'm doing anymore. I'm lost.'

And would you believe what I said next? I said, 'I think I need God.' No one had ever preached the gospel to me nor shared the love of Jesus Christ but those words just tumbled out of my mouth: 'I think I need God.'

By the age of twenty-six I had been living in a vicious cycle for ten years, trapped in a life of drug and alcohol addiction, and I couldn't find my way out. My life had come apart at the seams.

I had been a child star and had grown up working on two iconic Australian TV shows. One was called *Young Talent Time* and the other was called *Neighbours*. *Young Talent Time* was Australia's version of the US television show *The Mickey Mouse Club*. Every Saturday night at 6 pm, ten teenagers and the host of the show, Johnny Young, brought the hits of the day into your living room. *YTT* was on Australian television for twenty years, and had a massive viewing audience – it was a phenomenon really. From a young age I just loved music. It was always my dream to one day be on the show. Never in a million years did I ever think that would become a reality.

I had grown up in Tasmania singing in music class and school plays. By the age of twelve my brother Brett and I put together our own band with a couple of our best friends. I was a huge Kiss fan back then. I had a dream of one day becoming a famous lead singer in a rock band. Eventually I started writing my own songs and was encouraged by a girl in my music class to enter a local talent quest. In the talent quest I sang an original song and was awarded the 'encouragement award' and was then placed into the grand final. I was so excited about it!

Leading up to the grand final I was told that one of the judges was a producer of *Young Talent Time*! I nearly choked. All of a sudden the talent quest became a big deal to everyone. It no longer felt like an isolated local thing; it became something so much bigger. Twenty-five acts had been placed in the grand final and some of those acts were established bands and singers so, really, I felt like I had no chance. The whole thing felt kind of surreal to me.

I was the last act on stage that night. I was only thirteen years of age so by the time I got on stage it was way past my bedtime! I remember being so nervous because there were at least two thousand people in the audience. Back then that was like Wembley Stadium to me! That night I sang Michael Jackson's song 'Ben', and it went down an absolute storm. I actually ended up winning the talent quest, which became big news in Tasmania. On the Monday morning I was headline news on the TV and my face was splattered all over the front page of the papers!

A few weeks after winning the talent quest my mum and dad were called by the producer of *Young Talent Time*, who was a judge at the talent quest, and I was offered the opportunity to fly to Melbourne, Australia to audition for my favourite TV show. Wow! Things were becoming even more surreal. It was like someone had hit the forward button on a remote control and everything in my life had sped up all of a sudden. I couldn't keep track.

My mother and I were flown from Hobart to Melbourne, then picked up at the airport and driven to the *Young Talent Time* head offices. I remember being totally awestruck when I met Johnny Young, the host and creator of the show. I had watched him on TV ever since I was a little boy and now he was standing right in front of me. I nearly wet myself because he was there for my audition! Again, I sang Michael Jackson's song 'Ben' and was stopped half way through the song. I thought I'd done something wrong but Johnny Young just looked at me and my mother and said, 'Mark, we'd love it if you could join the show and become a *Young Talent Time* team member.' I was speechless.

Actually this opportunity was a huge thing for my family because it would mean uprooting everyone to give me the chance of a lifetime. I remember my parents having some pretty intense discussions around that time regarding the possibility of moving. After a week or so my parents came to a decision.

It was a 'Yes!' So, as a family, we moved and set up camp in Melbourne, Australia. We didn't realise that we would be there for the next seven years!

I worked tirelessly on *YTT* whilst also trying to fit into a normal school routine. I loved it. Each year the team would tour Australia doing huge concerts in every major city: Sydney, Melbourne, Brisbane, Adelaide, Perth and Hobart, with sometimes seven or eight shows back to back in each city. Pretty amazing when you consider that there were twelve thousand people at each show! We were chased down the street by fans at every turn and a lot of the time couldn't even venture outside without a bodyguard. I worked with Australian household names like Dannii Minogue and Tina Arena. But after nearly four years I felt like it was time to move on.

I wanted to try something different so I got myself an agent, thinking they would help me with my singing career, and they got me an audition for an Australian soap opera called *Neighbours*. I auditioned for the part of Nick Page and won the part up against forty-four other young actors. For those of you who watched the show you might remember that my character, Nick, was caught by Henry and Todd spraying graffiti on Jim Robinson's workshop fence. Nick would eventually be taken under the wing of Helen Daniels (Anne Haddy) who felt a connection to him because her character, too, was an artist. The two characters would build a strong bond together and after the passing of Nick's grandmother, Nick would be asked to move in with Helen and the Robinson family.

I had never tried acting before and don't profess to be a great actor by any means but, I must admit, I loved working on the show. I built some strong friendships with the cast during the two years that I worked on the show. I had the opportunity to work with Jason Donovan for a whole year up close and also had the privilege of working with Guy Pearce for two years. Guy was always an outstanding actor who was destined for great things in the industry.

In its heyday (1987–1992) *Neighbours* had a viewing audience of around twenty million people worldwide. The shows impact on places like the United Kingdom was so extraordinary, in fact, that it caused the country to grind to a halt each lunchtime so that people could watch their favourite soap opera. *Neighbours* was instrumental in opening up a wider world platform for me. It enabled me to travel extensively, working in theatre and recording music in the United Kingdom. I was asked to sign a record deal with BMG and was managed by Kenny Smith, who also managed The Eurythmics. I worked with Nik Kershaw on my first record and toured with bands such as Take That to promote it. I rubbed shoulders at parties with George Michael, Mick Hucknell and Elton John. I loved working in the entertainment industry. It had been my whole world for many years.

THE SLIDE

From a young age I was always curious of what it would feel like to get drunk or take drugs. Behind the glitter and glamour of my TV career, I was getting high *a lot*. The entertainment industry is full of temptation. I had been surrounded from a young age by adults who frequently used drugs. In my early teens I experimented with alcohol and marijuana with industry friends. By the age of seventeen I then progressed to using speed and LSD. Then by the age of eighteen I was experimenting with cocaine and ecstasy.

At the age of nineteen I moved to the UK, which was twelve thousand miles away from my parents, so things quickly became crazy. I started earning huge amounts of money, hence my drinking and drug-taking went to a whole new level. I was no longer buying one gram of cocaine, I was buying ten grams at a time. I was no longer buying one pill of ecstasy – I was buying fifty pills at a time and offering them as hors d'oeuvres at parties. My cupboards were literally filled with bottles of whiskey and beer. This was the first time I had lived by myself. There were no boundary lines so it was time to party! I was nineteen years of age, young and naive, and I thought everyone had the best intentions for me, but how wrong I was.

After meeting the wrong people in the UK my life began to slide downwards. I started listening to their voices regarding the direction my career should go, and then made some foolish decisions which didn't go down well with the record company. The record company lost interest in me and I lost interest in them. My career took a back seat and the party life took a front seat.

Before I knew it I was gripped in a life of addiction and I

was on a fast, downward spiral. I would turn up to recording sessions completely 'out of it' and would not be able to sing nor achieve anything. I remember turning up to the photo shoot for my album cover and spending most of the time vomiting in the toilet. I would then do a line of cocaine and pep myself up so I could at least function. I started to look a complete mess. The signs were beginning to show and people were noticing.

My home life in Australia wasn't helping either. After being in the UK for a long time I returned home to find that my family was going through personal challenges that were incredibly difficult to find any resolve in. This caused me to drift away from my family and estrange myself even more. Trying to find the truth at that time was like grasping at the wind.

A deep anger was brewing inside my soul, so much so that I hit out at my father one evening and we came to blows. It was awful. My mother's heart, like so many times before, was completely broken and she was left to pick up the pieces. After that I fled the scene for quite some time and stayed with friends.

Bitterness and resentment were eating me up inside and I couldn't run away from them. Everything in my world was falling apart and the way I dealt with it was by taking more drugs and escaping. I isolated myself in a drug-fuelled world and ended up depending so heavily on them that I would befriend anyone who could supply me with my next fix. I loathed who I had become.

I moved back to Australia for quite a few years and toured

around the country in cover bands. I struggled to get my life together. My addictions had so gripped me that life became all about earning enough money to stay high.

I remember jumping out of a moving taxi one morning coming home from a nightclub. I had been partying for three days straight with no sleep. I became so paranoid and claustrophobic that I literally bailed out of the taxi! With cuts all over my arms and back I was taken back to my friend's house where I proceeded to overdose on cocaine. My friend saved my life by dragging me fully clothed into an ice-cold bath and then, by screaming at me and repeatedly slapping me in the face, she managed to get me breathing again – but it was touch and go for a while.

In many ways I had experienced so much so quickly and wondered if life had anything more to offer me. My soul was empty. I was searching – searching for some kind of sense to my world through the addiction and mess, but I couldn't find any answers. My heart had been broken in so many ways by relationships and career let-downs. I was desperately looking for life's meaning but I was looking in all the wrong places. I remember asking the same question to myself over and over again, sometimes out loud in a drunken stupor: Did this life have anything else to offer me beyond the things I had experienced?

Eventually I went full circle and ended up living back in Tasmania with my parents. They moved back there for a quieter life. Eventually they told me that part of their reason for moving was because they didn't know what to do with me anymore. I had sold everything I owned at this stage and really just needed a roof over my head, so my circumstances had forced me to move back in with them.

After moving in I visited a few nightclubs in Hobart and bumped into a couple of guys who were party animals just like me. We got high, talked and decided to get a three-piece band together. We started gigging soon after we met. I was pretty much wrecked all of the time at this point in my life. I was also battling with depression and failure and did everything not to face them.

I remember performing in front of crowds of ten or so people in little pubs in Hobart, Tasmania, completely stoned and drunk. I couldn't even talk let alone sing. I remember on one occasion falling off the stage and not being able to finish the music set. People just pointed their fingers at me and shook their heads in disgust. I was fired by the management of every place I worked in.

So there I was, back where it had all began. I was twenty-five years of age. In the world's eyes I had had it all and lost it, and in many ways that was the truth. But who knows that truth as the world sees it is not God's truth?

ENGLAND, HERE I COME AGAIN!

My brother Brett was also living in Tasmania at that time because his marriage had unfortunately just ended. One day he came to visit me and said to me, 'Right'o, mate, here's what we're going to do. I'm sick of this crap here. I'm going to sell my car and buy you and me a plane ticket back to England. What do ya reckon? Are you coming or what?'

I didn't need to think twice about it. I said, 'Bro, I'm already there!' Within a couple of days we were on a plane headed back to London, England.

When we arrived we had arranged to move in with an old friend of mine. Brett and I got a plan together and set out to demo some songs. Things were going okay for about a month; we were building some momentum and meeting new people but, again, the grip of addiction was so strong that it pulled me away from all that we were doing.

After nine months or so my brother was totally fed up. He ended up moving back to Australia because he couldn't handle watching his little brother destroy himself. When Brett went home things went from bad to worse.

I became friends with a guy who, unknown to me, had a heroin addiction. We went back to his apartment one evening to smoke some dope and cocaine mixed together. When we were high he said to me, 'Hey, Mark, have you ever chased the dragon?'

I thought he had gone completely mad. I said, 'You what?'

He said, 'You know, have you ever done any heroin?'

I quickly said, 'No way.' I hated needles and just the mention of the word *heroin* sent shivers down my spine. I had seen a few of my friends get completely messed up on it and one even lose their life.

He said to me, 'Hey, it's cool, you know. You don't have to

shoot it. I just smoke it. It's not as addictive. The high is totally wild. I've been doing it for months and I'm fine.'

I became curious. For some reason the thought of it caused my heart to palpitate. I felt my mouth go dry and my stomach knot up.

My friend went to his bathroom and lifted up a piece of carpet, under which was a little bag with brown powder in it. He bought it into the lounge, sat down on the couch and went through a small ritual. He took a small amount of the powder and placed it on a piece of foil, put a handmade cylinder in his mouth and then carefully heated the foil up underneath. He waited until the heroin started to melt and then as smoke began to rise he breathed the contents into his lungs. He instantly sat back on his couch and breathed out a sigh. I watched the pupils of his eyes dilate and shrink as small as pin pricks. He looked over towards me and said, 'OK, man, it's your turn.'

Time seemed to go into slow motion as I considered the opportunity. Alarm bells were going off inside me but they were counteracted by the thought of, 'Well, things couldn't get any worse so why not?'

Looking back on this moment I can almost see the devil sitting on the edge of his seat, wringing his hands in glee, not daring to breathe as he waited for my response. My response was, 'OK, let me try it, just this once.'

That was it. Before I knew it I had stooped to an all time low and was selling stolen CDs to Cash Converters to support a heroin addiction.

My daily pattern consisted of waking around lunchtime, rolling a joint and heading down to Cash Converters to sell some CDs. I'd make around £40 to £50 on the exchange. I would then make haste to my local pub where I would have several beers while I waited for my dealer.

I would pick up my gram of heroin and make my way back to mine or a friend's place to 'chase the dragon'. On the odd occasion when I couldn't afford heroin I would drink a bottle or two of cough medicine to get high. I just wanted to escape and dull the pain. I didn't care much about eating so I just did it when I had to. At this point drugs were much more important.

Towards the end of my dark road I was hanging out with some very heavy individuals. I witnessed drug deals where guns were carried. I could have lost my life on one occasion as a drug exchange went horribly wrong but, by the grace of God I am still here.

I became suicidal, deeply depressed and was also a very violent man. I was often in fights and was banned from entering several establishments in West Hampstead, London. I eventually lost all respect for myself. My complexion became pale and bloated and I often vomited because of the state my body was in. Most mornings I would wake in a sweat with the shakes, needing my next fix.

During this very dark time I met a Christian girl and we started dating. She had one foot in the church and one foot out of it and wasn't really following God with her whole heart. We met in a dark, dingy little bar in West Hampstead. It was like one of those late night bars that you see on the movies, where you knock on the door and a man on the other side of the door pulls a slat back and rudely says, 'Who is it? What do you want?' It was a complete dive of a place. God knows what this girl was doing there! She just *happened* to be an Australian girl who had grown up watching me on television. Go figure that! She was in the UK working in the entertainment business as Michael Barrymore's personal assistant.

Because of my addictions our relationship was very short lived but for some reason she remained a friend in my world and would often visit me at the pub I frequented. I didn't know it at the time, but after we broke up she returned to church and, along with a group of friends, started praying for me. Now, that church happened to be Hillsong Church in London. Hillsong is one of the most influential churches in the world for its music. It would soon be my home church for the next four years of my life. It would also be the place where I would have the opportunity to travel all over the globe singing for Christ. And it would be the place where I would meet my future wife, Bethan.

CHAPTER 2

A CHANGE IS COMING

After my ex-girlfriend and I broke up, I later found out that she went back to church and got her life right with God again. And as I said, I was also told that she and a group of friends were praying for me.

It was around this time that a shift started to occur in my life. Normally I was completely self-absorbed – that's what a drug addict is like, they're just concerned about getting their next fix. But all of a sudden I found myself feeling a deep empathy for people. I would talk to people for hours about their lives. These were people who normally sat by themselves in the pub drinking themselves into oblivion. I befriended an old lady and found out that her husband had recently passed away. She was totally broken-hearted and would drink her sorrows away. I went to visit her husband's gravesite with her on one occasion. I just stood next to her comforting her as she wept over his grave.

In the Easter of 1996 my mother called me out of the blue and forcefully told me that she wanted me to visit a church and 'say a prayer'. She made me promise that I would. I promised her just to get her off the phone but, the weird thing was, I felt compelled to go to church! I couldn't shake the thought.

After convincing a friend of mine, they ended up driving me to find a church so I could fulfil my promise to my mother. When we pulled up outside I said to my friend that I'd only be a minute. I remember walking inside the old church and seeing a small group of people in the bottom right-hand corner praying and singing. I sat at the back listening to them for at least half an hour feeling a warmth wash all over me. All of a sudden I was startled as I heard a car horn beep outside and then realised that my friend was still waiting for me! She wasn't very happy when I returned to the car.

One summer's evening, as the sun was setting, I was on my way to the pub and coming towards me was a priest. Our eyes locked and we both stopped on the footpath just staring at each other. It was like he just knew I was going to speak to him so he stopped to wait for me to find my thoughts. I had such a surreal conversation with him.

I said, 'Hello.'

He replied in a posh London accent, 'And hello there young man.'

I noticed that he had such a peace and ease about him. I just stared at him for a while and then said, 'Um. I've been thinking a lot about my life lately, you know.'

He curiously answered me by saying, 'Oh you have? And how so?'

I was quite apprehensive, but managed to say, 'I've been thinking lately that surely there must be more to life than just having a family and a career and then you get old. I mean, that's all good but there must be more to life than that.'

He didn't hesitate in answering my question, but he answered in a way that left me curious and hungry for answers. He said to me, 'Oh you're so right there, son. There is so much more. All you need to do is find out what that more is.' And then he smiled at me and walked off.

I remember just standing there on the footpath, feeling this warm glow come over me, and a sense of excitement rise up inside me. As I walked towards the pub all I could hear in my head over and over again was, 'There is so much more. There is so much more.' I thought about what he had said for days, it was driving me crazy! I would sit at the bar next to people and ask them if they knew what the 'so much more' thing was all about but nobody had a clue.

My ex-girlfriend and her church buddies must have been praying hard because what happened to me next completely rocked my world.

I was on the Kilburn High Road in London with a few friends one afternoon. This was early August 1996, just weeks before my encounter with Christ. I had just bought an apple at the local fruit and veggie shop and for some reason I felt compelled to wash the apple. Now, I don't know why that stands out in my mind so strongly, but it does. Normally I would have just eaten the apple but for some reason I had to wash it, so the manager allowed me into his private kitchen to do so. After I'd given it a rinse I walked outside the shop to join my friends and was completely taken aback by what I experienced.

All of a sudden it was like a layer of reality had been peeled back and I was presented with a deeper form of reality. I instantly knew what people were burdened with just by looking at them. It was like I had the ability to look into their souls and understand what was troubling them. I was shocked by what I saw. I sensed a lot of hatred, hurt and torment. People's judgement towards one another and their eyes of criticism swept over me like a flood. It was like the pain of their souls was revealed in my hearing. The wind was totally knocked out of my sails and I froze. As I stood there, more of this experience started to unfold. I instantly knew which sickness and infirmity people were carrying in their bodies. It was like a veil had been drawn back and I was seeing through a different set of eyes. To tell you the truth I thought I'd gone totally mad. I now know that what was happening to me was called the 'discerning of spirits', which is a spiritual gift that God can at times impart to people. I remember saying to my friend next to me, 'Are you seeing what I'm seeing?'

He just looked at me strangely and said, 'Mark, what are you talking about?' I was speechless and unable to explain to him what I was witnessing so I just stood there motionless. My friend put his hand on my shoulder and said, 'Mark, are you alright?' After a few moments the experience lifted and things went back to normal but I was completely messed up by what I had just witnessed. I then remember walking towards the pub dumbfounded and confused and not able to communicate with anyone.

I THINK I NEED GOD

The night before my encounter with Jesus Christ and being confronted by my ex-girlfriend, I remember sliding down the wall at her house, cupping my head in my hands and saying these words, 'I think I need God.' With no rhyme or reference those words just tumbled out of my mouth.

My ex-girlfriend said to me, 'Mark, I don't want you to go back to where you're staying. I want you to stay here tonight. I believe that if you go back to where you're staying I don't think I'll ever see you again.'

I remember saying, 'Don't be silly, I'll be fine.'

Again she was strong with me and said, 'No, Mark, listen to me! I want you to stay here!'

I said, 'Alright, alright, calm down, I'll stay.'

I must have slept for about four hours, but then I awoke shaking uncontrollably. A drug addict calls this 'the rattles'. I was so sick – so sick, in fact, that I asked my ex-girlfriend to take me to hospital. I thought I was going to die. I had vomited all over my clothes and couldn't stop. I ended up vomiting blood and bile. I was in such pain. I remember her wiping me down with a cold flannel, wiping the vomit and sweat off me. I also remember her reading psalms from the Bible and speaking in some weird language that I couldn't understand. I couldn't make out what she was saying. After an hour or so I started to feel a little bit better but I was so cold. I had taken my vomit-stained clothes off and wrapped myself in a sheet for warmth. So, there I was, wrapped in a sheet, sweating and shaking.

And then all of a sudden, it happened.

> *On the morning of the 26th August 1996 God broke into my world. My life was shaken and transformed* ***INSTANTLY!***

The atmosphere of the room suddenly shifted and I knew without any doubt that I was sitting in the presence of God! After coming to the end of myself, and exhausting every option, I met my Saviour. Jesus Christ. In a moment of time He came into my life and saved my soul. In an instant He removed and destroyed the many addictions that had held me bound for so many years. His presence flooded the room that desperate summer's morning and I began to cry out to Him, 'Oh God. Oh God. I'm sorry, I'm sorry.'

His presence was so tangible and strong that it literally felt like electricity surging through me. Everything in my being knew that Jesus Christ, the Son of God, was in the room with me! Don't ask me how I knew. *I JUST KNEW.* I know that sounds strange but it's the truth. There was Someone incredibly powerful in the room with me. I might not have been able to see them, but they were definitely there.

Instantly I was changed from the inside out. I felt power surge through my body, a power so strong that it literally took hold of me and shook me to the core. It was like someone was pouring liquid love all over me. I was immersed in it. I became detached from the place where I sat and was literally taken into the awareness of another place. No drug had ever taken me this high before.

Without a doubt I knew that God actually existed and nobody could ever dare take that away from me. I broke down and cried for hours and hours as I called out to Him. I wept for so long I didn't think I would have any tears left to shed. As I wept I felt God's presence surround me. I could sense His face right next to mine. I could feel His presence so intimately.

Through my tears it suddenly dawned on me that His eyes had seen all. Everything I had ever done, the good and the bad. He had seen me as a little boy riding my bike for the first time. He had witnessed my birthday parties. He had watched over me and protected me night after night while I slept. But then He had also seen me in the nightclub toilet, snorting my first line of cocaine. He had watched me smoke heroin off foil. He had watched me do things that still cause me to break out into a cold sweat if I remember them. And despite all of it, He still loved me. I couldn't get my head around it. But my heart knew that He had come to show me the way out of all the mess I had sadly wrapped myself up in. He washed over me, again and again, and I couldn't stop crying. Through my tears I kept repeating, 'I'm sorry, I'm sorry.'

A few days after my encounter with Christ it dawned on me that I didn't have any desire for drugs. Now that felt totally weird because I *needed* them. My body cried out for them. I couldn't go more than a day without some kind of drug in my system. My body would shake and sweat and I would get incredibly angry. I thought to myself, 'Could it really be that I am free of my addictions?' I didn't want to drink alcohol either. Alcohol was like an old friend of mine who had kept me company for years. We knew each other well. He had given me a false sense of courage and happiness. He had helped me escape so much heartache. But now I didn't want to be in his alluring company anymore. I didn't need a cigarette either! The thought of inhaling smoke into my lungs seemed like the dumbest thing in the world to do. Why would I want to pollute and violate the strength and purity of my vital organs? And I noticed that I couldn't even bring myself to swear or curse! I mean, I had a filthy mouth. Every second word I said was a swear word. But now the thought of any of these things actually repulsed me. I realised that I had been *SET FREE!* I was so thankful, so grateful. I was overwhelmed that my addictions had been broken! All I could do was thank God. Wow!

I soon regained enough strength to visit the pastors from London Hillsong Church. I had no clean clothes to wear so I was given some by my ex-girlfriend's next-door neighbour. They were way too big for me but, hey, I didn't have any other options at the time! I remember walking into the Hillsong offices in London and being introduced to a man called Pastor Steve Maile. He took one look at me and said, 'Wow, you've definitely been touched by God, haven't you?'

I remember looking at him saying, 'Yes. I definitely have!' We had quite a lengthy conversation about my life and then he asked if he could pray for me. I immediately said, 'Yes.'

No one had ever prayed for me before; at least, not in front of me.

He got up from his seat and moved around the desk towards me and said, 'OK, Mark, close your eyes and lift your hands to heaven.' Well, before I could do what he had asked me to do I felt that same presence that I had felt a few days ago surge through my whole body. But this time it literally swept me off my feet! I tried to steady myself but I ended up falling backwards into a pot plant in the corner of the room! I was so shocked by this that I didn't know what to do! A presence that I could not see literally just passed through me! I was helped up by Pastor Steve and he said to me, 'You have nothing to be afraid of, Mark. What you're experiencing is the presence of the Holy Spirit. It's OK.'

After a while I was able to stand up again but I felt heavy and kind of drunk at the same time. Suddenly there was a knock at the door, and Pastor Steve answered it. It was the Worship Pastor of the church, a guy called Mark Griffiths. Pastor Steve invited him in and introduced him to me. I must have looked so weird to this guy. Not only had the Holy Spirit just knocked me out, but my clothes were way too big for me and I felt completely drunk! I was still coming to my senses.

Pastor Steve asked me if they could both pray for me once again. I said, 'Um, yes, that would be great.' Again, the same thing happened to me! I was completely knocked out by the presence of the Holy Spirit. I ended up on the floor this time and was so overwhelmed by His presence that I couldn't stop crying. I lay there on the floor for at least ten minutes as God's presence washed over me again and again. Gosh! What a way to be introduced to church!

That day Pastor Steve and the Senior Pastor, Gerard Keehan, immediately arranged for me to move out of my ex-girlfriend's house into an apartment with two young guys who had had similar encounters with God. We instantly became great friends. After moving in with them I started going to church straight away. I felt like I had come home, it was overwhelming. I was incredibly impacted by the worship and the preaching. My heart was ready to soak in all that God had for me. I had an insatiable hunger for God's presence and His Word. My new flatmates and I would pray for hours and hours, every spare moment we had would be spent seeking God. We prayed and fasted and often took communion together. I wanted to know this God I had just met; I couldn't get enough of Him.

MY FIRST TIME LEADING WORSHIP

The first time I stood on a platform to lead worship was at Hillsong Church in London in late November 1996. I'd been a Christian for three months. Now, I'd been singing since the age of three and, as I said, had worked in the entertainment business for many years, so performing was like second nature to me, and standing in front of an audience was no problem at all. But this was different. I must say the first time I stood up to lead God's church in worship I was afraid. Scared out of my wits! Why? Because this was no longer about me; this was about Jesus. I was afraid because I felt the huge weight of responsibility on my shoulders to lead God's people into a holy place, a place where they would encounter the living God. I was no longer entertaining. I was ministering in the power and presence of the Holy Spirit. Wow! And that's a totally different mindset to adapt to so I wanted to get it right. There was no more 'taking a bow at the end of the song'. There was no more trying to look cool in front of my fans. No, this was me leading people into an encounter with Jesus so their lives could be changed in the way that mine had been!

This was so much better than entertaining. I had stumbled upon the very reason I had been given the gift of being able to sing and I understood why I had been given a passion to write and play music. It was for this reason: TO WORSHIP GOD AND GOD ALONE. What a magnificent and high calling! What a joy and what a privilege to be able to use sounds and melodies to glorify the King of kings, and to join with the angels in blessing His holy name! Hallelujah!

Well, after that first time leading I never looked back and I knew that I wanted to lead worship all of my days. Anything else would be a downgrade to me from the privilege of leading people into an encounter with Jesus.

> *All of my days I will sing of Your greatness,*
> *All of my days I will speak of Your grace,*
> *All of my days I will tell of Your wondrous love*
> *Your love in my life, Your love.[1]*

VISITED BY ANGELS

It was a Saturday in May 1997 where, after worshipping God for several hours, I was visited by angels. I had entered a realm in worship that was truly breathtaking. All of a sudden the atmosphere radically shifted. I then became aware that the music I was playing was being drowned out by the most beautiful sound I had ever heard. I was shocked and in awe because I knew instantly that I was in the company of angelic beings. Although I couldn't see them, I could hear them. God's presence became so heavy that I stopped playing the piano and then fell off my chair sideways onto the floor. As I lay there I listened to antiphonal voices sing over me. I wept like a baby as I listened to this sound, a sound that I had never heard before. I knew there was more than one angel in the room, it sounded like several. Their voices sounded like the most perfect voices I have ever heard, split into harmonics that were beyond anything a human voice could create. Their voices seemed to glow and circulate, ebbing and flowing. The depth and beauty of the sound they created was beyond description. The presence of God was so strong that I could not stand so I just continued to lie there weeping. Then after a while the sound slowly disappeared and I was left there speechless, dumbstruck.

Later that evening, when my flatmates returned home, I tried to communicate what had happened to me, but they just looked at me with strange eyes and nodded their heads and said something like, 'Wow, that's awesome, Mark.' My life was so transformed that day. I knew even more so that there was a spirit world, a world alive and active that we can't see with our natural eyes. I became aware of God on another level from that day forward, and the insatiable hunger I had for Him became even stronger.

1. 'All of My Days', words and music by Mark Stevens, ©2000 Hillsong Music Publishing

CHAPTER 3

SOLD OUT AND NOT AFRAID

"How beautiful are the feet of those who preach the gospel of peace, who bring glad tidings of good things."

Romans 10:15

One of the first things I learned about being a Christian was that some people aren't going to 'get you' – but I also learned that I couldn't let that stop me!

I remember calling my father on the phone a few days after my encounter with Jesus Christ, trying to explain to him what had just happened to me. I was so blown away by what had taken place that I couldn't wait to share it with him. I remember saying over the phone excitedly, 'Dad, I've just met Jesus!'

Immediately the wind went out of his sails and he replied in disbelief, 'You just met who? Oh no, Mark. You haven't become one of those weirdos, have you?'

Shocked, and still trying to be excited, I said, 'Um, no, Dad. But I have had an encounter with Jesus!'

He pulled the phone from his ear and shouted to my mother, 'Sandy, you better come and talk to your son. He's saying he's just met Jesus!' Not really the response I was looking for. I had it all made up in my mind that my father would be absolutely over the moon for me, but how wrong I was.

I can't blame my dad for his response. It must have sounded crazy to him. The son that he had previously known as a heavy drinker and drug taker, the son who had lived an excessive lifestyle for many years was now claiming to have met Jesus! A bit hard to get your head around, don't you think?

It took me a long time to realise that my father was walking his own journey with God and that because of his past experiences he'd arrived at some faulty decisions about Him. I'm praying that his perception changes because I know God has such an incredible plan for my dad's life. It still makes me smile, though, thinking about his response to the best thing that's ever happened to me!

In the Gospels Jesus encourages us by saying, 'If you will confess My name in front of men, I will confess your name in front of My Father' (Matthew 10:32, my paraphrase). Praise God! That's an incredible promise to hold in our hearts, the understanding that each time we talk to someone about our faith in Christ, Jesus has a conversation with His Father about us! Now that just makes me want to shout His name from the rooftops!

WHERE ARE WE?

I saw God do one of the most powerful things, in terms of His presence working through me to impact others, early in my walk with Jesus. I had been invited to sing at a bar in Soho,

London. Now this was about six months after my radical conversion experience with Jesus, so I was still very new to my faith. A guy who used to attend church approached me after a Sunday service and told me that each weekend he was responsible for hosting a singing competition at this bar he worked at. He said that he would love it if I could sing one of the gospel songs I had recently written and also asked me not to come alone but to bring a friend. I was a bit apprehensive to say the least because God had only recently saved me out of a life of drug and alcohol abuse, so frequenting bars and nightclubs was something I historically did on a nightly basis! Even so, the thought of singing a gospel song to a bunch of unsaved people excited me, so I agreed to go.

The following Friday night my friend and I went to the bar. Once inside we were shocked by what we encountered because we had actually been invited to a gay and lesbian bar. I said to my friend, 'What on earth have we been invited to? Should we get out of here?'

My friend said, 'No, Mark, you should do what you came here for: you should sing.'

Now I had grown up in the entertainment business, working with gay people since the age of thirteen, but I was newly saved and had only just begun to process my relationship with God, so I must admit I felt extremely uncomfortable. You can imagine the scene: there were men embracing men, and women with women; I didn't know where to look, so at times I just stared at the floor! After what seemed like an eternity I was invited up to sing. The atmosphere was noisy and rowdy and the smell of alcohol and cigarette smoke was in the air. As I walked towards the stage I remember that everyone was just staring at me. As I stepped behind the piano I looked up at everyone and nervously adjusted the microphone stand. I took a deep breath and said, 'Hi, my name's Mark, and I'm going to sing you the first song I ever wrote for Jesus.'

At that moment, a heckler shouted out, 'Mary!' Not really a great way to start. But I began to sing:

> *There are so many souls in a wander land, far from home,*
> *Lost and torn inside from their past, you can see it in*
> *   their eyes.*
> *But there's a place where we all can be,*
> *All you have to do is believe,*
> *For in this graceless age,*
> *We can all turn the pages,*
> *And praise God's own Son,*
> *Jesus, O Jesus,*
> *Son of Man, You are the one,*
> *Jesus, O Jesus,*
> *Son of God, You are the one for me,*
> *For all eternity.*[2]

As I was singing, the presence and power of the Holy Spirit filled the room and everything just stopped. You could have heard a pin drop as people watched and listened intently. And this was in a packed out gay and lesbian bar! I was amazed.

As I was singing I remember looking at people's faces thinking how lost they all seemed, like they were desperately searching and so in need of God's love, in need of answers. After I finished my song there was silence but it wasn't an uncomfortable silence, it was a warm silence. Then, after a long moment, people started to clap and cheer. That really threw me. People were actually touched and didn't hesitate in rushing up to meet me and introduce themselves. Their response was amazing. Several people even said (and remember these are unsaved people) that they saw angels standing behind me as I was singing! That really blew my mind because why would people make up something like that? I mean these were lost people with no God conscience whatsoever. Both my friend and I had the opportunity to share our stories with several people that night. There was such a hunger for God in those that we spoke to. I was very moved by what took place.

To cut a long story short, I sang another song that night, which was 'Amazing Grace', and won the singing competition. Then, after being handed £50 by the manager, we were swiftly asked to leave the premises. Weird. I think he was totally convicted by God's presence. It was such a surreal experience. I will never forget that night. The Holy Spirit shows up most powerfully in the darkest of places.

STAND UP!

Daniel was a man who stood up in his generation and was

counted. In the face of great opposition and resistance he chose to worship God in public view despite being told by the law that he couldn't.

King Darius had been persuaded by his staff to pass a law that all in the land were to worship him only – a man! They were not to bow down to any other gods. The king's persuaders were men who were fighting for power and position and were jealous of the excellent spirit that resided in Daniel. They couldn't find any fault in Daniel so they focused on his relationship with God and sought to set him up by passing this law.

To his own danger Daniel chose to wholeheartedly disobey the king's decree and continued worshipping God in full view of everyone. And not just once but three times a day! An incredibly bold act considering the penalty would be death. It makes me laugh because some of us are too afraid to share our faith with our neighbour!

Daniel was a recognised man, he was an important man and his decisions carried great weight. I believe he was deeply aware of this and understood that it was his role and commission to set a standard for God's people. So Daniel chose to worship and obey God instead of a man, even if that man happened to be a king!

"You shall have no other gods before Me. You shall not make for yourselves a carved image – any likeness of anything that is in heaven above, or that is in the earth beneath, or that is in the water under the earth; you

shall not bow down to them or serve them. For I, the LORD your God, am a jealous God, visiting the iniquity of the fathers upon the children to the third and fourth generation of those who hate Me, but showing mercy to thousands, to those who love Me and keep My commandments."

Exodus 20:3-6

Because of Daniel's direct unwillingness to bow down to king Darius and worship him as his god, he was thrown into the lion's den! Now we can probably all think back to a few occasions in our own journey where we have been ridiculed and criticised about our love for Jesus, but that pales into insignificance in comparison to Daniel's situation. This was a whole other level. I think Daniel's circumstance lets us know that on occasions our worship of Jesus Christ can place us in a difficult position, to say the least! A position where we'll need to choose between God's way or the world's way.

The beautiful thing we see in Daniel's situation is that *God protected him* in the lion's den and He will protect you, too. When we choose to worship God in difficult circumstances I believe God makes it His business to show up in an unusual way.

The next day, when king Darius' guards pulled Daniel out of the lion's den, not a scratch, not a lion's paw print was found on his body! Whoa! Why? I believe God was pleased to use Daniel as an example, because of his unwillingness to bow his knee to someone other than God.

When we bow our knees to anything other than God we are effectively worshipping the enemy. Deep in his heart I believe Daniel had a revelation that God would bring to nought the plans of the enemy because he chose to worship and obey Him. God shut the mouths of lions on his behalf and God will do the same for you and me. I encourage you to be bold in your expression of worship! Don't draw back! God will honour you as you continue to honour Him.

Now we might not have to face literal lions in our lives, but we may have to share our faith with people who possibly won't understand. Or we may have to stand in a room full of gays and lesbians whose lives seem to be anything but God-fearing and share our love for Jesus Christ. So I pray we'd be sold out and not afraid!

I believe there is someone reading this book who is in a lion's den of hopelessness and discouragement and you desperately need lifting out. There are others who are in a lion's den of despair at the loss of a loved one. Others who are over their heads in debt and financial turmoil, and yet others battling addiction. Well, let me encourage you. I pray that as you begin to call out to God right now you will begin to receive a realisation that God is your Protector, Provider and the Lifter of your head. Everything you will ever need is IN HIM, every answer and every breakthrough. He is your exceedingly great reward. I pray that He would impart to you strength and a heart of praise so the heaviness that you have felt upon your life would be broken and lifted. I pray that you would again find faith in His promises and an understanding that He WILL and CAN do what He has promised. His Word WILL NOT FAIL! I send this word into your lion's den in the name of JESUS. May you rise up and live a life that is *SOLD OUT AND NOT AFRAID!*

2. 'You Are the One', words and music by Mark Stevens, ©2014 Mark Stevens Music Ltd

CHAPTER 4

THE REAL WORSHIPPER

*"For [as far as this world is concerned] you have died,
and your [new, real] life is hidden with Christ in God."*

Colossians 3:3 (AMP)

When I became a follower of Jesus Christ I hardly had any sense of myself. But as I began to read God's Word and spend time in His presence I discovered that I was God's beloved son. I realised that He loved me deeply, had known me before I was born and had a specific purpose for my life. He had pre-written and pre-arranged a plan for me. That blew my mind! The fact that I had been thought about before my conception – not just by my incredible parents but by the Creator of the whole universe – was breathtaking.

I also found out that I was a joint-heir along with Jesus Christ to the awesome promise of a kingdom that was being revealed in the hearts of men called 'The Kingdom of God'. Wow! I was a royal son! I was a part of something so much greater than I could have ever imagined. In God's eyes I was a somebody; a somebody that He loved despite my own faults and flaws; a somebody that He had destined to crown with His favour; a somebody that He had included in His eternal plan.

So, when I met Jesus my mission began, and that was to seek out who I really was. I sought to uncover what God held in store for me in this life. I had sold myself into believing that what you see is what you get, but that was far from the truth. Just like the ocean and its depths, my real life was waiting to be explored. There was so much more to be realised and only the real and authentic me could possibly find out what that was. I had to get on my knees and spend time with the God who had saved me. I had to touch His heart with my heart and ask Him, 'Who am I, really?' I needed to know. I got desperate about it. I embraced only those around me who could push me into that place, and I shut off every other hindering voice that would try to stunt me and slow me down. It may have seemed rude to some but I didn't care anymore. You see, life had dished me up so many lies: the lie that I would be dead by the age of twenty-seven like some of my 'so called' heroes; the lie that I had no hope and no future; the lie that I was an alcoholic and a drug addict and that would be my lot; the lie that I would never experience the love of a wife and the birth of my own children. Man! I had believed so many lies. But, after meeting Christ, the old me died and was buried in the sea of forgetfulness and the new me came to life. The real worshipper had arrived! I was done with the old, it was dead and rotten and it stank. I had to unwrap the new me in Christ and enjoy the beauty of what the new me had to offer. The new possibilities, the new horizons. The new friendships with people who were on the same mission who, too, wanted to discover in greater degrees the real worshipper that was within them.

As I began to immerse myself in God I surrounded myself with people who knew Him intimately. They each became leaders to me spiritually. I began to understand that there was something incredibly unique about them. They were what I called 'Real Worshippers' because they had within them the innate ability to awaken the real worshipper within me. In Christ they had discovered who they really were because the reality is, only in Christ can we find our real self, our true and authentic self. Like the scripture says at the beginning of this chapter, 'our true and real life remains hidden *in Christ*'.

I believe a real worshipper is a spiritual catalyst who causes those around them to be inspired to go after God with everything.

A real worshipper continuously longs to discover new postcodes in God. And they don't just visit, no, they unpack their stuff there and are seeking to move in and live on higher ground!

When I was a boy I remember being in the family car with my mother, father, brother and sister, and we would drive into million-dollar neighbourhoods and excitedly look at million-dollar homes. My parents would dream about one day moving into the area. I would wind down my window, catch the breeze and wonder what it must feel like to run around in a house that size. It must take whoever lives there hours to run from one side of the house to the other! And what would they do with all that space? I mean, how many televisions did they have?! They must have twenty kids to have a house that size!

Then we would drive past another house and another and another before exiting the estate and heading back to our house. We visited and then left because we weren't owners.

As I have followed leaders whom I consider real worshippers, I have come to understand that the spiritual postcode they live in has come at a very high price. It has cost them everything to live in the liberty they now possess and they have the battle scars to prove it. They have had to fight for the change that others enjoy. They were the ones who had to disempower strong controlling individuals so that the next generation could be empowered to find their voice. They had to learn to bless those who cursed them and pray for those who dragged their name through the mud. They were the ones who stayed up all night and prayed on behalf of others until they got their breakthrough. They were the ones who carried the financial burden of building multi-million-dollar facilities so that others could enjoy them. They were the ones who broke new ground in order to possess the things we now take for granted. They had to learn to choose love and not embrace bitterness, choose grace instead of judgement, choose to not settle for 'good' in order to reach for the 'great' they held in their heart.

Many people look at a real worshipper's life and want what they have, but if they really knew what it cost to enjoy it, they would not have enough in the spiritual bank account of their soul to pay for it.

A real worshipper lives from their heart and not just their head. They are a person who is moved and governed by the real and authentic them and not the socially acceptable person everyone else would have them be.

So often in life we end up living someone else's version of it, being forced into a role, a career or a way of thinking that is unbecoming to who we essentially are. Because of this we live much of our lives frustrated and unfulfilled. Frustrated because we know in our hearts that we're not doing what we know we were born to do. If not dealt with, this frustration can later lead to resentment and anger. So it must be our life's mission to find our real worshipper within!

A real worshipper is sensitive to 'atmospheres'. They will not allow themselves to comply with a system that seeks to drain them, keep them small and dominate them negatively. They will not allow their heart to be stifled nor tamed. They know deeply that they are called to break out of and break beyond what is perceived as 'normal' by others, by inwardly transcending their environment. This is not done in a rebellious way, no, but rather in a spirit of leadership, strength and faith.

The real worshipper is therefore an 'atmosphere setter', whether in a home, a classroom, a business or in a church, it really makes no difference where. A real worshipper will by nature seek to change the spiritual climate for the better.

I believe everyone is aware of 'atmospheres'. Atmospheres can be felt. They are tangible. If you're used to a certain atmospheric climate, one that's full of life, fun, laughter and belief, and then you step into something that is completely the opposite you almost instantly recognise the difference. You may even feel a sense of claustrophobia or mood change. Some atmospheric changes are subtler, but they are still noticeable. A real worshipper's focus is to quickly deal with the spiritual climate and shift it into a more positive climate. They may even become indignant about it. They have within them a certain strength and liberty of heart that breaks any form of heaviness, restraint and control. This is done so others can enjoy an atmosphere that is representative of heaven.

I think we need to understand that every person is responsible for creating his or her own atmosphere. We create the atmosphere and make it palatable for God to move within. The Bible tells us that Jesus could do no mighty works in his own hometown Nazareth due to a lack of faith. Faith was the governing element that would have enabled the Son of God to move in power. But because people were familiar with Jesus and did not see Him as the Son of God they could not receive from Him. Remember, it was His own hometown. A lot of people would have seen Him grow up around them and would have shrugged Him off as being 'Joseph's son' and thereby dulled down Jesus' ability to impart to them. God is very sensitive to atmospheres, too! May we give Him room to move by creating a climate that is pleasing to Him.

A real worshipper is by no means an entertainer or a performer, no, they are not a crowd pleaser who is there to do a show. We live in a world that is infatuated with entertainment and performance and sometimes we fool ourselves into thinking a powerful performance is called 'the anointing'. But the anointing is not given to leave us all sweaty with a warm, fuzzy feeling inside. The anointing is manifested to break the yoke of the enemy and to usher people into an encounter with a real and living God. Don't get me wrong, I love to be entertained, I enjoy a good movie and love going to concerts, but I know the difference between great entertainment and the power of God. A real worshipper brings the power of the Holy Spirit into the equation and not just a well-rehearsed performance. They usher in the presence of Christ and people's lives are transformed!

I have been in many, many church meetings, but I have to say the meetings that I remember most are the ones where I've been led by someone who is ministering from their heart. You see it's so easy to go through the motions in a church setting, getting caught in the structure and framework we create whilst failing to hit the mark when it comes to connecting with the heart of God and ministering to the people. We have 'the form' of a church service going on but somewhere along the line we've edged Jesus out of the equation. We're doing the work of the ministry but have left no room for the Minister of the work. I believe a real worshipper makes it their business to ensure that the structure and framework serves and facilitates what God is doing, not what they are doing. Now I realise that a service must be ordered and planned to some degree, but my prayer is that we would leave some room for spontaneity!

When David danced with all his might (2 Samuel 6), I believe he was simply responding to the cry of his heart in that moment. I have no doubt that this was a spontaneous thing that overtook David. It's moments like these that you can't plan.

You may be able to relate to this, but I remember working in a team setting on occasions where we would plan everything down to the last note and, I have to admit, it absolutely killed me. I hated it. Something in me wanted to mess it all up and throw it out the window! I was thinking to myself, 'This is all wrong.' I mean how can you plan the purity of real worship? Sure, we can prepare ourselves and have a plan because we want to effectively serve our congregations. I get it. There needs to be some kind of framework. But I pray that we would not be so planned that we fail to allow spontaneous moments into our set-list or messages or, for that fact, anything we do! Otherwise our lives and churches just become clinical, sterile and highly predictable.

IT MUST HAVE BEEN TOTALLY SCARY, HANGING OUT WITH JESUS . . .

. . . because you never knew what was going to happen next! I mean on the first day of His ministry the religious crowd tried to throw Him off the brow of a hill because He said something that offended them! Great first day at the office, eh? Jesus couldn't even attend a funeral without messing it up and raising someone from the dead! Brilliant! And at night, while His team slept, He enjoyed defying the laws of gravity by walking on the water! Jesus constantly did things that kept people on the edge of their seats.

So let me ask you a few questions. Are you excited when you attend church? Are you on the edge of your seat when listening to the preacher? Or do you know exactly what to expect? Are you bored? If the answer to the first two questions is NO and the answer is YES to the second two, then something is wrong. God seriously wants to rock your world!

I don't doubt for a second that when Jesus' disciples woke up each morning they said nervously, 'I wonder what He's going to do today? What on earth is going to happen?!' I think at times they felt like leaving Him and going fishing again for a safer and more predictable life. But how boring would that have been? Especially after experiencing the things their eyes and ears had witnessed!

I believe a real worshipper has learned to live outside the opinions of what others think they should be, and what others think they should do. Now this may sound rebellious but hear my thinking on this one.

There's a passage of scripture in Mark chapter 5 that talks about a man called Jairus. When Jairus sought out Jesus he had an incredible need in his life, he was in desperation. His little daughter was lying at the point of death! Jairus was a very important man in his community but on this particular occasion his importance could not help him. We are told that he fell at the feet of Jesus and begged Him earnestly to visit his house, that Jesus might lay hands on his daughter so that she might be healed. Jesus was moved by Jairus' faith and followed him to his home where He was prepared to perform a miracle. As they were on the way to Jairus' home they were met by two men on the road who Jairus obviously knew well. The men had come to inform him that his daughter had died and that he should not bother Jesus anymore with his desperate request. Can you imagine the fear that struck Jairus' heart? His little girl, naturally speaking, had just died. It was at that very moment that Jesus looked at Jairus and said these words to him, 'Do not fear, only believe.'

You see, Jesus knew that He had within His hands the power to heal Jairus' daughter. He was willing and able to perform a miracle in the girl's life. But would Jairus continue to believe Jesus or would he choose to believe his friends? Jairus was caught at a crossroads. He could either believe the natural reality of his circumstances or he could choose the higher reality of Christ's words. Thank God Jairus chose to believe Jesus! And because he chose to believe Jesus he received a miracle. His little daughter was raised up and Jairus' family was restored! Hallelujah!

I'm reminding you of this story because a real worshipper has learned to choose the truth of God's Word over man's perspective, even if man's perspective seems like the truth. Jairus' choice to embrace Jesus' perspective must've looked crazy to his friends who informed him of his daughter's death because, in their eyes, things looked hopeless. But they were looking through natural eyes, not supernatural eyes. A real worshipper understands that they must find their supernatural eyes to see with, even in the face of incredible adversity and misunderstanding. Having the ability to see what God sees causes them to get what God has. And that's exactly what happened for Jairus, he got what God had for him. The real worshipper within him came alive!

I have purposely said that a real worshipper is a 'worshipper' because worship is an essential part of who God has made us to be. The reality is that we all worship someone or something. Worship is simply about who and what we value the most. I remember Louie Giglio speaking about worship once; he said, 'Following a trail of your time and energy will give you a great understanding of who and what you value the most.' That's a sobering thought.

You see, worship is all about holding someone or something in the highest regard. A real worshipper has therefore decided to hold God's precepts, principles and presence in the highest regard, understanding that this will ultimately lead them into favour and blessing and that following God beyond the opinions of man will cause them to live a life that defies the odds! They have come to the conclusion that they would rather be in trouble with people than miss what God has for them.

Worship is about intimacy. It is the pathway that enables us to find out who Jesus essentially is. It's the bringing close of the divine and the creation. Being intimate with Jesus causes the real worshipper to see a part of God they would never get to see in the company of others. I don't know about you but, depending on who I'm with, I reveal different levels of who I am because of the quality of that particular relationship and the trust I have with that person. It's the same with Jesus. Through worship we have the opportunity to build a depth and quality of relationship with Him that is different to our relationship with others. And it's in that place of intimacy that we begin to bump into who He really is, and who we really are. Again the Bible says in Colossians 3:3 that 'our true life remains hidden in Him'. If something is hidden, friend, then it's up to us to go and find it. Yes, it's up to us to dig for gold. This is what a real worshipper has done and continues to do. They are on a constant quest to find the real them in Christ who is created in the image of God.

I now realise that I have been instantly drawn to real worshippers all of my life. I remember watching TV with my mother as a boy, I can't have been more than four years of age, and I would be overwhelmed with emotion as I heard a gospel choir sing. Other people sang and it was nice but when I heard a gospel choir I would stop in my tracks and would start to cry. I now understand that my little boy's heart was being touched by 'the sound of real worship'. Inside me there was a spiritual connection going on. I was inwardly drawn to the sound of heaven. It was as if my uninhibited boy's heart had the ability to hear a spiritual sound that my head could not grasp. I have come to the conclusion that God was awakening me to real worship even then.

Throughout my childhood God surrounded my life with

a handful of people who knew Him well. Although at that time I was unaware of their faith, these people had a profound impact on me as each of them had living within them the hallmark of being a real worshipper.

I absolutely adored my Pre-school teacher. She was my teacher for two consecutive years. What I came to understand, as I got older, was that she was the senior leader of a church, married to a man of God. Back then I was far from ready to receive Christ as my Saviour, but I think it's interesting that I was completely taken by her. She had such a soothing and calming effect on me. As she would read stories to the class I would wander off in my mind and bring her words to life. Being in her presence gave me a sense of safety and security.

My dad's younger brother, Peter, had a great impact on me, too, as a boy. I had no idea during my younger years that he was a Christian; I only found this out once I had my encounter with Christ. But it explains so much to me because he was always exciting to be around. He was funny and full of life and was a genuinely good person. Like me, God had rescued him out of a life of drug abuse. What I later found out when I spoke to him, after my encounter with Jesus, was that he had been praying for me when I had been going through that very dark time.

I visited him in Tasmania on several occasions and we had the privilege of worshipping God together. We sang together, read God's Word, shed tears of joy and also laughed a lot as we enjoyed God's presence. I don't think it's by coincidence that my mother and father asked him to be my godfather and I don't think it's an accident that we both share the same middle name. We were the first two salvations in the Stevens family on my father's side! Isn't that awesome!

As a teenager I loved the band U2 – and still do by the way! I have seen them play live on many occasions. Bono fascinated me, and the charisma he had when he was performing was totally mesmerising. Being a songwriter from a young age, I would read his lyrics and be very curious about the deeper meaning of them. There was one song in particular that stood out to me called 'Who's Gonna Ride Your Wild Horses' on the *Achtung Baby* album. The lyrics awakened something inside me to start asking questions. Bono's lyrics describe his heart as an empty lot, left vacant for any spirit to haunt. It caused me to question whether or not there was a spirit world. I then started to read books about Bono and discovered that he was a believer in Christ. I thought his faith was interesting to say the least. Another song that messed with my head was 'I Still Haven't Found What I'm Looking For', a gospel-based track on the *Joshua Tree* album. The lyric that stood out to me the most was where Bono says that, even after speaking with the tongues of angels, and holding the hand of the devil, his heart was still as cold as a stone, it still hadn't found what it had been looking for. Again, I wondered what he meant.

A little later I found out there was a heavenly language called 'tongues' that God supposedly imparted to people, but I'd never heard anyone speak in it. And had Bono really held the hand of the devil? Is there a devil? I mean, I had played on the ouija board as a kid and had seen the glass move across the board. I thought, 'Maybe there is a spiritual realm! Maybe there is a devil, and maybe there is a God.'

It sounds funny, I know, but God used these things to awaken questions on the inside of me.

During my time at Hillsong in Sydney, Australia, Darlene Zschech had a massive impact on my life. Darlene is unquestionably one of the greatest catalysts in the realm of praise and worship today. And not just a catalyst in praise and worship but in helping lead the charge for God with a passion to raise up the next generation of real and authentic worshippers of Jesus Christ. Darlene carries within her a flame for Christ wherever she goes and is only interested in ensuring that people encounter God and bring the honour that is due to His name. I remember her encouraging and provoking the church in countless meetings to understand that 'worship is not a performance, it's a command and we should do it with all of our hearts'! I loved standing next to her, locking in with the momentum and power she displayed when leading worship. It was breathtaking. I learned so much!

Darlene has a heart within her that longs to see the lost find Jesus, the broken restored, justice given to the mistreated and marginalised, and she also desires to see communities rebuilt and restored. She loves God and loves people. Now, that is someone that we can follow! She is a real worshipper.

I believe that God has designed it so that all of us are born with an inner compass or GPS system which lets us know when we're doing the right thing or when we're doing the wrong thing in terms of living out our divine purpose. You see, life has a way of dulling down our awareness of that inner GPS system. Life has a way of drowning out the voice that will help guide us towards our real worshipper. But, if we learn to listen, we can again find that voice.

The Holy Spirit is always speaking, always coaching you, always offering sound advice in order to guide you towards your greater purpose and plan for being on the earth. So it's our job to consistently 'tune in' to His frequency and live from that place. Real worshippers know how to dial up Radio God! They are people of prayer and worship. They are people who know how to praise God. They love the Word of God and have an insatiable hunger for the Holy Scriptures. They know when to get away and how to get away to hear the voice of the Holy Spirit.

The Bible tells us in 2 Chronicles 16:9,

> *"For the eyes of the LORD run to and fro throughout the whole earth, to show Himself strong on behalf of those whose heart is loyal to Him."*

He looks for real worshippers to hand His precious promises to because He knows that whatever He passes to them will be valued and carried out with the right heart and in the correct manner. You see, God wants to bring heaven to earth! But

He has no way of getting heaven into these earthly streets without those who carry heaven and are saturated with heaven in their hearts. He has no other way of revealing the kingdom of His beloved Son to those who desperately need Him.

More recently I was teaching a classroom of students on the baptism of the Holy Spirit. God's presence was powerful. I felt totally free and was flowing in the authenticity of my real worshipper. I spoke in tongues at the end of the session and then God gave me the interpretation. A few students were offended by me speaking in tongues, because they came from more conservative denominations and therefore aired their disapproval to their friends. Well, somehow news travelled back to me and I was a bit gutted, to tell you the truth, because I believed God had really moved in the session. It was actually arranged that I was to speak with the same class the very next day so I thought I would bring to light that I had heard a few people were offended by what had taken place. Here's a brief summary of what I said to them when I stood before them.

'The title of my message today is 'Don't Fence Me In'.

'Ladies, what would you do if an angel of the Lord showed up to you and announced that you would be impregnated by the Holy Spirit and would give birth to the Son of God?

'And gentlemen, what would you do if you were walking home one evening and you saw a burning bush that somehow wasn't being consumed by the fire. In your curiosity you draw closer to it to check it out and, to your absolute surprise, the bush starts to audibly speak to you about your destiny and future?

'And what would you all do if you saw a man casting demons out of a crazed lunatic that everybody has heard about in your town? Then the man proceeds to instruct the demons that possessed the crazed lunatic to be sent into a herd of pigs. It gets better – the man then shouts at the pigs and orders them all to run into the nearby lake, and all the pigs are drowned!

'And what would you do if you saw a little boy giving a sandwich and a piece of fish to a man who then takes his small offering and miraculously feeds four thousand people with it?

'Lastly, what would you do if you were attending a funeral and a man walked in and rudely disturbed the sombre mood by touching the coffin and causing the dead person to come to life?'

The faces of the students were all confused, but I think I had their attention.

I then said:

'These are but a few miracles in the Bible that we often mention without a second thought and they are all scriptures that we supposedly base our life of faith on. But let me ask you a question: if they showed up in your world today how do you think you'd react?'

Again there was quiet.

'I came into class yesterday and prayed in tongues and then gave the interpretation to what I believed the Holy Spirit was saying and encouraging us in, but I heard that some of you were offended. To tell you the truth that really concerns me because, to be honest, if what I did offended you, I really don't think you're ready to be used by God at all.'

Now I really had their attention.

'The reality is, ladies and gentlemen, God will not live in our quiet, cosy little boxes. God will not be fenced in by anyone or anything! He is not a socially acceptable God. He is not trying to fit in. I believe those of you who were offended yesterday need to ask yourself 'why'. I think you need to grow, and grow quickly, and I really hope that during your time at this academy you learn to embrace a few more ideas other than the ones you're currently familiar with. I honestly don't think God wants you to live a safe life. He is far from being a safe God! He is God in all His freedom and authenticity. So let's commit today to not fencing Him in and let's definitely commit to not fencing each other in!'

The word on the street was that people's lives were impacted and changed.

Let me say this to finish this chapter. The truth is, we are all real worshippers but some of us have not found that person within us in all its fullness yet, or some of us may not have found that person at all. Or you may have found that person and you're completely resonating with the things I have said in the chapter. That's brilliant. Whichever it is, the fact is God's desire for all of us is that we might truly know and become accustomed with our real worshipper, with who we authentically are. The real us – with the quirks, leanings, passions and desires that make us unique. Some of us may need to peel back several layers before we can catch a glimpse of that person.

You may need to take off several masks of characters you've created to please others before you bump into that person. You may need to say and do some things that you know will get you into trouble with other people before you can find your real worshipper! You may need to separate from friendships that hold you back and control you before you can find your real worshipper. But I encourage you to do whatever it takes to find the real you! It will be the most liberating thing you ever do.

Friend, you have something to give to this planet that is unlike any other person. You have something to say in all its authenticity that will change someone's life or that may even affect a nation's future. But while you are still holding onto the fear of what others will think of you, you will never find yourself in all your fullness. There is greatness in you, but that greatness emanates from the core of who you are. Don't be frightened and don't be afraid. God wants to liberate you. It may freak out your family and your friends when you liberate the real you, but that's OK, they are used to the person that conforms and complies. But hey! This is a new day. It's a new time for you. It's time for the real worshipper to be awakened and set free! You are a REAL WORSHIPPER!

CHAPTER 5

ME?
FIND TIME FOR GOD?
YOU MUST BE KIDDING!

Reading this book is a miracle for some of you. You're spinning so many plates right now that it's virtually impossible to find time for you. Your life is filled with so many commitments, challenges and complexities that you think, if I dare stop for a minute, everything will just crash down around me. I know how it is, believe me.

I used to work three jobs whilst still giving 120 per cent commitment to my local church, Hillsong Church in Sydney. I'd wake at 6:30 am each morning and catch a bus to the coffee shop where I co-managed to open up by 7:15 am I would then finish my shift at 4 pm, race home and freshen up so I could be at the restaurant by 5 pm where I worked as a waiter. I would finish there at 10:30 pm and then leg it to the supermarket where I would pack shelves from 11:30 pm until 3:30 am I did these three jobs four days a week and then for the remaining two days in my work-week I did only two jobs so I could at least get a few hours sleep!

Beyond that I would serve at church and sing my heart out

in up to seven meetings across the weekend. I would also rehearse on a Wednesday night with the creative team. Three times a year, for nearly a month, I had the privilege of singing backing vocals on albums until the early hours of the morning and then occasionally I would also have the awesome privilege of travelling to different countries with the music team to lead worship. The busy schedule we had on the tours was like a holiday for me! I kept this up for three years during my time at Hillsong Church in Sydney. By the end of three years I was absolutely fried! I didn't just have bags under my eyes, I had luggage! So, friend, if you're over-stretched, I get it.

ON THE GO!

Some of us have become professionals at making time for God on the go, not stopping at all to catch our breath. We throw on a CD in the car on our way to work and listen to some music or teaching while we fight our way through the traffic. We don't really worship, we SHOUT to the Lord, or maybe even at the car in front of us! We do our best to 'shabba-dabba-do' and pray in tongues as we burn fuel down the motorway. A few of us have even closed our eyes and forgotten where we are, almost running into the back of the car in front of us. Not me of course! Not.

The deal is, we live in such a busy age where so many things cry out for our attention that it's almost impossible to slow down. And when we do finally find a little 'me time', all we usually want to do is crash and burn. Or if we have a little bit of energy to expend, maybe even catch up on our favourite TV shows or go to the gym or, if we're married, go to bed early (if you know what I mean), that would take an angelic visitation for some married couples. Ha!

Some seasons in our lives are incredibly demanding. We, as parents, have children to take care of – that's a full time job in itself! We have friendships to build and nurture, careers to lead, jobs around the house to do, bills and taxes to pay, cars to have repaired, gardens to tend to, doctors to see if we have health issues, kids' extra tuition and hobbies to pay for, and the list goes on and on. Phew! I'm exhausted all over again. How 'bout you?

Now, dare I even go there? Should I take a risk and mention it? You might close the book but I may as well! Somewhere amongst all that busyness, in the midst of all the plate spinning, we need to make time for God.

Maybe you're saying, 'Mark, if you knew how crazy my world was you'd understand that it's virtually impossible for me to do that!' Well, my friend, you're definitely the one I would love to talk to in this chapter. Just give me a few minutes of your precious time to say some things that I believe will help you.

I believe it's vital as a follower of Jesus Christ to find time to pray and read God's Word otherwise we become followers of everything *but* Jesus. We become so immersed in our schedule and daily routine that somewhere along the line we edge Jesus out of the equation. He doesn't get a look in.

Now I know you're probably thinking, 'Well, Mark, Jesus is with me all of the time. He's omnipresent. I can talk to Him anywhere!'

Yep. I'm aware of that. But let me ask you a question: have you ever tried to have an important conversation with someone who's not really listening to you? Frustrating, isn't it? And have you ever felt that when you were giving away your heart, and you were saying things that really meant something to you, you weren't being listened to with the level of attention you needed? I think you get my point. There are times when God wants your full, undivided attention because He's got important things to say to you. There are times when God wants to talk to you about your future and about your decisions. He wants to encourage you in the unfolding of your destiny. He wants to talk to you about your family and what He needs you to give them emotionally and spiritually. God may want to give you some fresh ideas that will bless your world. But whilst you're trying to spin three hundred plates and have no time for *you* let alone *Him*, He can't say what He wants to say to you.

QUALITY, NOT QUANTITY

I remember hearing a great teacher called Joyce Meyer say something in her meeting that changed my life forever, and I immediately wrote it down. She said, 'The quality of your ministry is determined by the quality of your time spent with God.' Joyce was referring to how Jesus often drew away to solitary places to pray and spend time with God. Sounds nice, doesn't it? Some of you are probably thinking, 'I'll do it if there's a bed to crash out on!'

But what stood out to me was when she said 'the *quality* of your time' spent with God and not 'the quantity'. Some of us feel guilty because we are not able to give God the quantity of time that we think He deserves. We feel condemned because we once heard a well-respected preacher say that we need to pray four hours a day, three hours in tongues, thirty minutes in English and the last thirty minutes standing on our head reciting Psalm 23 backwards. So we live under a big, black cloud feeling that we're a failure and we've let God down. But, like Joyce said, I believe God is not after quantity, He's after *quality*.

Quality time is simply about you giving your best to God in the private time you have together. It's about you being 'all there' and not somewhere else in your mind. It's amazing what a few minutes of quality time with God can do for you. It can still your soul and rebalance you. It can refresh your mind and body and refocus you for the day ahead. And because of the results, making quality time with God will cause you to wonder why you don't do it more often.

Jesus understood that, for all He would face in His life and ministry, He would need to have a strong root into God to overcome the many trials and adversities. He also understood that in order for Him to be effective in His ministry He needed to be more aware of God than anyone or anything. The needs He encountered required having a different mindset and a powerful hook into heaven's resources. The success of Jesus' life would not just rest in His own strength and ability, but in the quality of His relationship with the Holy Spirit.

The hallmark of Christ's ministry was the inexhaustible display of God's fullness that each person encountered when they came into contact with Him. There seemed to be no limit to His capabilities towards someone with a heart of faith. You're probably thinking, 'How on earth does that relate to me, Mark?' Good question. Let me say this:

"Your success in life is based more in your relationship with God than your routine or schedule."

When we anchor our lives in a 'doing' mentality rather than a 'being' mentality we are headed for spiritual bankruptcy. Failing to nurture and feed your being, or your heart, will cause you to become burned out in 'the doing'. That's why we are called 'human *beings*' not 'human doings'. So, if your *being* is energised in God then your *doing* will become so much easier.

I love the scripture Zechariah 4:6 that says,

> "*'Not by might nor by power, but by My Spirit,' says the LORD of hosts.*"

In this scripture God was speaking to Zerrubbabel about the grace that would be upon his life in the work of building God's house. God was helping Zerrubbabel understand that the work of his hands would be blessed by the power of His presence and that there would be an awareness of someone so much greater working on his behalf.

Verse 7 of the same chapter goes on to say, 'Who are you, O great mountain? Before Zerrubbabel you shall become a plain!' Again speaking of God's ability to make something that is potentially huge and daunting look like nothing to Zerrubbabel! My point is: allowing God, through relationship, to work in the midst of our doing causes us to achieve so much more.

The beautiful thing about being a believer in Jesus Christ is the fact that we are not on our own. We have a Helper and Friend called the Holy Spirit walking alongside us all of the time. But the reality is, a lot of us don't ask for His help because we are too busy! Kind of ironic, isn't it, that the Helper is willing to help us, but we are so busy helping ourselves, and others, that we forget to ask Him for help!

Spending quality time with God will energise your being and will cause you to get in touch with the broader reason of *why* you do what you do. The thing that always energises me in the routine of life is that there is the promise of a greater life for me in God. There is the promise of eternity with Him. There is a God that I can talk to and pray to. He is a God who is intimately acquainted with all of my ways, who is deeply concerned for me. What also energises me is having a revelation of the hope that He has placed within me, the hope of a victorious life here on earth, filled with purpose, promise and provision for both myself and my family.

A LIFE OUTSIDE OF THE SYSTEM

It's so easy to get caught up in serving the machinery and systems of life. We work within organisations, ministries and businesses that require a level of service from us. They demand our time, devotion and labour, and rightly so. But what we must understand is that in order to stay energised and joyful in what we do, we have to experience a life *outside of the system* so we can effectively serve the system. We have to enjoy a flow apart from the system otherwise the system will eat us up and spit us out. That may sound harsh but it's true. When you build anything from an organisation to a ministry it will demand huge levels of commitment and energy from you and will not care whether you're fit or unwell. It has requirements and demands that continuously shout for you! So you need to create a way to fill the tank of your life with fresh fuel on a daily basis. And just as fuel empowers a car, the presence of God will empower you.

> *"You shall receive power when the Holy Spirit has come upon you."*
>
> **Acts 1:8**

The word 'power' in the scripture above comes from *dynamos,* which is the Greek word from which we get the word *'dynamite'*. I encourage you, if you need to find a little dynamite or explosive, rearranging power in your life, just spend quality time with the Holy Spirit! He is the essence of power and He

88

is the source of strength.

Jesus is the greatest leader that has ever walked the face of this earth. He fully understood that He had to have an intimate relationship with the Holy Spirit to empower all that He was doing. He knew that He needed a life that was separate from the control of the many systems and social structures He walked amongst. That way He could bring change and liberty to those who lived under the influence of them. Jesus offered a better way to people, a higher way. He did not promise that everything would be rosy or without trouble, but He did promise the awesome privilege of having a relationship with His Spirit in every moment of every day and He did promise the reality of a little piece of heaven in your earthly experience!

GOD IS A GOD OF CHANGE, AND HE WANTS TO CONSTANTLY UPDATE YOUR WORLD

The beautiful thing I have discovered about walking with the Holy Spirit is realising that I'm never going through anything alone. And I'm man enough to say it! So often in life I have tried to do things in my own strength and have failed to realise that I have God living within me to strengthen me, equip me, bless me, empower me and direct me.

At times I have become so immersed in the many responsibilities I have that I have left no room to talk to God about them. So I have fallen into ways of doing things that worked for a season but then those ways quickly became old and outdated, yet I keep doing them because they worked yesterday. But God wants to speak to us about finding ways to change our world that will best serve us NOW. I believe He wants to help us lessen the load so we can have a better quality of life.

I am discovering in my life right now that it's not about 'how much' we're doing as much as 'what' we're doing. When you essentially find out 'what' you're meant to be doing and with whom you're meant to be doing it, there will be an element of grace and joy attached to it. There will also be a *much bigger harvest of blessing and results* involved because it's *in keeping with your deepest passions and desires*. Personally, when I do anything that's attached to my calling or purpose, which involves music and communication, I yield much greater results than anything that's not in keeping with it. Now it's taken me a long time to reach the season I'm in, but I must say I'm a much happier and fulfilled person doing what I'm doing. Do I work hard? Yes. Do I get tired? Yes. But there is a sense of joy and fulfilment that comes along with the tiredness that brings satisfaction to me.

VISION-BASED, NOT ISSUE-BASED

Before I finish this chapter I want to share an experience with you that I know will help you.

More recently I've had the privilege of working with several different ministries as a consultant. What I normally do when I begin with a ministry is to meet with the senior leadership team to understand where their frustrations lay and where they need help. If it's a church I'm working with I attend a Sunday service to assess what's going on. If I'm working with the creative team I also attend a rehearsal to see how they go about things. I will then go away and create a plan and strategy that will enable them to move forwards.

In one particular ministry, I was working with two gentlemen who were responsible for heading up their church worship team as Worship Pastors. They weren't employed by the church but had been a part of it for nearly twenty years. Both had families and both worked in demanding jobs outside of the church.

They were responsible for leading a large team of around sixty people, both pastoring them and teaching them, whilst also covering the practicalities of creating song arrangements, rota systems and ensuring that the team had online resources and materials to stay ahead of the game.

When I mention 'pastoring' I mean 'counselling and encouraging' the team they lead. Pastoring can be incredibly draining and time-consuming because, let's be honest, people's lives can be messy and complex. Even rota systems can be a huge task when you're trying to accommodate sixty people's diaries! So, that was a lot of work for them to be doing outside of their family commitments and full-time jobs.

When I came onto the scene I walked into a lot of stress. I saw how hard these two Worship Pastors worked in order to ensure their Senior Pastor's requirements were met with a high level of excellence. But I also saw how burned out they were and how 'issue-based' their ministry had become. They were too burdened to think about anything beyond their issue-based leadership, like the broader vision of the church, not to mention their own personal goals.

Over the next few weeks I also learned how frustrated the team was. The team seemed stuck and bored and looked desperate to get their hands on some of the action. They were full of gift and the ability to help but there seemed to be a huge chasm between the Worship Pastors and their team, not due to any pride but due to a lack of relationship because of busyness and stress. There was no time for the Worship Pastors to build any kind of qualitative relationships with their team; they were too busy and heavily burdened! I needed to help them quickly.

After meeting with the Senior Pastor to discuss what I had seen, I presented a plan to him that I thought would ease some of the pressure and inspire growth. I then met privately with the Worship Pastors and said to them, 'You know, I really think we need to create a team of carriers around you two that will help you share the load. That way you can empower and grow the next generation of leaders that will soon take this ministry forwards with you. What do you think?'

What happened next was not the response I was expecting. They both welled up with tears. I must admit it was a bit over-whelming to see a couple of grown men become so emotional! They actually couldn't get their heads around the fact that they were worthy of being helped and served. They had been too afraid to ask their team because they thought they might say, 'No.'

After encouraging them and giving them a little bit of wisdom, the guys approached their team and asked several people to get involved in helping them carry the load. People jumped at the opportunity and things changed very quickly, both in their personal lives and in the team. A weight lifted off the Worship Pastors and a sense of joy came back to the team in a matter of weeks because people felt a greater sense of involvement and value.

Over the course of a few months, new leaders were raised up and, as a result, creativity started to flourish. New ideas were beginning to come to the fore. In a matter of months the team began to write their own songs. Then new doors of opportunity opened up for them to be able to minister in other churches and conferences. Sunday services became a pleasure rather than a chore. Over the course of twelve months, because the stress had diminished, people were added to the team because it looked like a fun and exciting ministry to be involved in. You attract what you are! Things quickly went to a new level.

IT'S TIME TO READJUST THINGS IN YOUR WORLD

I tell you this story because it may encourage you to readjust some of the things in your world to enable more time for you. Beginning to work a plan where you can delegate some of the responsibility to others will change your life and maybe even save your ministry or organisation. Or it may simply help you let go of some of the things that are weighing you down.

I really pray that this chapter has helped you if you're overly stretched or completely stressed out, or maybe that's not the case for you. You may just need to adjust a few small things. Wherever this finds you, I know that God is asking you to make *quality time for Him*. I believe He has some new things He wants to say to you that will help you in the next season of your life. God doesn't want you to stay as you are. There are greater things for you to push into and experience. But God is going to ask you to let go of some things that you think you need, in order to fly higher. And when you do let go you'll find that they weren't yours to carry in this season, it was someone else's responsibility to carry them. Remember:

> "*The quality of your ministry (LIFE) is determined by the quality of your time spent with God.*"

CHAPTER 6

THE PRESENCE OF THE HOLY SPIRIT

In these next few chapters I'd like you to come with me on a journey while I unpack some thoughts about the presence of God. Ever since the day I was saved I can truly say that I have had an insatiable hunger for God. There is nothing more beautiful in this world to me than His presence.

Before I met Jesus I experienced a lot of things in my life, but nothing would ever compare to what I've found in Him. His presence is more precious to me than the rarest jewel. It is my highest prize. And being able to walk intimately with Him this side of heaven leaves me speechless at times. I am awestruck and incredibly thankful to know and enjoy the presence of the Holy Spirit in my every moment.

> *"The Spirit of the LORD is upon me . . ."*
>
> Luke 4:18

When Jesus Christ walked the dusty streets of this earth people would come from miles around to hear Him speak. People were desperate to get near Him, to touch Him, to be impacted by the presence of the Holy Spirit that He carried. The Bible tells us that Jesus carried the presence of the Holy Spirit without measure. There were no limits to what God was able to do through Him. The power and presence of God rested upon Him in such an inexhaustible degree that anything, yes, anything was possible! I can see it now: chaos ensuing as lepers, blind men, tax collectors, prostitutes, people with loved ones who lay at the point of death, sinners of all kinds and all classes, desperately pushed towards Him to be seen and heard. They knew that He carried the answers they longed for. He had within Him the wisdom they needed for the vicissitudes of life. He offered the reality of an eternal kingdom that brought with it restoration, joy and the promise of everlasting life.

The Holy Spirit working through Jesus was able to reach into the darkest hallways of people's lives, pushing past the hurt and beyond their shame to free their burdened souls. He was able to powerfully and lovingly infiltrate the human condition to break the chains that shackled their hearts and minds. His presence rendered helpless the work of the enemy and reached across time-past into their aching history, to liberate their today, so they could be free to build a stronger and brighter future.

Jesus is the Word of God who became flesh to dwell amongst us. Yes, God Himself walked this planet amongst us in human form! Jesus Christ was the declarer and the announcer of God in earthly glory, the literal sound-alarm of heaven itself! When He spoke the Holy Spirit would fully back His every word. He would send His word into the dark alleyways of this world and the Holy Spirit would run swiftly alongside it to touch the person it was aimed for. The Word and Spirit worked in complete unity. There was no disorder in their partnership. There was no disloyalty, just complete honour for one another. Perfection working with perfection. God in Word working with God in Spirit.

The only requirement that was needed for those drawing from Jesus was *faith*, for without faith it is impossible to please God. Faith was the golden key that unlocked heaven's door, enabling the King of kings to walk in. People needed faith in their hearts to receive their miracle. If they came with eager expectation their lives would never be the same again.

But let me say, not one of the miracles that Jesus performed would have been possible without the presence and power of the Holy Spirit honouring His Word and honouring His touch. Jesus understood more than anyone that flesh and blood could not bring the level of change that was needed for the issues that confronted Him. The depth of need that beat upon the door of His life was beyond the ability of any human hand to fix. He, like us, needed and relied upon the presence of the Holy Spirit to do the work of setting the captives free. He, like us, needed the Holy Spirit to show up and honour His Word, otherwise heaven's change could not occur. The Holy Spirit, the third Person of the Trinity, was therefore a vital presence in the life and ministry of Jesus Christ.

After Jesus was baptised by John the Baptist in the river

Jordan, we read in Luke chapter 4 that He was led into the wilderness by the Holy Spirit. It was there that He fasted forty days and forty nights and was tempted by the devil. After His temptation, and victory over it, He returned to His hometown Nazareth as a different person. We are told that He returned in the *power* of the Spirit. This is when Christ's ministry began to take flight. He was filled with such power and authority that news about Him spread throughout the streets like wildfire. There was such a flame resting upon His life that it burned up any trace of the devil's work that came near Him. The dead were raised, devils were cast out, lepers were cleansed, the blind were made to see, deaf ears popped open and lives were radically transformed. The power of the Holy Spirit was moving, confirming the Word through accompanying signs!

And NOW? Because of the death and resurrection of Jesus Christ and the sending of His Holy Spirit to us, you and I have the opportunity to do what Jesus did. To live like He lived. We have the opportunity to walk as He walked! Jesus announced in John 14:12:

> *"Most assuredly, I say to you, he who believes in Me, the works that I do he will do also; and greater works than these he will do, because I go to My Father."*

Friend, this is our time to *take our turn!* It is our watch and our opportunity to take the Word of God at face value and wholeheartedly walk in it, believe it and see it come to pass. Yes, it's our time to expose the fruitless works of darkness and bring the light of the kingdom of God into every town, city and village we live in. This is the greatest moment in history. We have more airways, outlets and avenues in which to tell the glorious news of the gospel than any of our predecessors. I believe the Holy Spirit is prompting us to think bigger and move quicker because where there is faith and unbridled momentum there is Holy Spirit action!

ABUJA, NIGERIA

A number of years ago I had the privilege of attending one of evangelist Reinhard Bonnke's crusade meetings in Abuja, Nigeria. Six hundred thousand people gathered to hear Bonnke preach. Yes, well over half a million! And let me tell you, that's a small crowd compared to some of the meetings he has done and is doing! People had come from miles around by foot, meeting together on a dusty field in the middle of nowhere. They had come to hear the Word of God preached and to draw from the powerful anointing that rests upon Reinhard. The lame were carried on stretchers, people in wheelchairs were there, the blind and the deaf had come and even the dead were brought by loved ones in hope of them being raised to life! Many were there to reach out to God for a miracle.

It was at this crusade that I met a man called Daniel Ekechukwu, who had been raised from the dead under Reinhard's ministry. Daniel had been dead for three days before his wife had brought his dead body to a crusade meeting to be prayed over. Daniel's car had careered down a hill and crashed. He had impaled himself on his car steering wheel, broken the bones in his chest, pierced his internal organs and bled to death. As he lay dying in the back of an ambulance, his spirit was taken out of his body by two glorious angels to heaven and to hell where he witnessed things that boggle the human mind. I listened to him passionately preach his story to the massive crowd of people, urging those who did not know Jesus Christ to give their lives to Him. The power of God's presence was so thick as he preached that I could barely stand it, in a good way! Hallelujah!

The meeting had begun at 4 pm with waves and waves of praise and worship, followed by powerful prayer taking dominion and authority over the works of the enemy. The worship team would sing for an hour and then swap over with another church worship team and the meeting would carry on. Again, waves and waves of praise and worship and powerful prayer taking dominion over the works of the enemy. Wow! This went on for four hours! You had to be there to feel the full effects of God's presence and power in that meeting. I mean, these people were not messing around! This was warfare and exaltation of the Most High God in its fullest form! It was incredible to witness. The people danced and sang with all their hearts – all six hundred thousand of them! It was a sea of praise.

By the time Bonnke stepped onto the platform to preach the atmosphere was set. We had broken through every cloud of spiritual heaviness and had entered a place where God's presence was absolutely electric. The place was pregnant with possibility. Reinhard explained to everyone what he believed God held in store for them. God was ready to pour out His love and miracles to His children. Bonnke preached – his anointed words still ring in my ears to this day – he shouted, 'Tonight, I feel like I'm twelve feet tall! I feel like a mighty lion! Tonight, the Jesus that is knocking at the door is the Almighty Jesus that has all power in heaven and in Nigeria.' The sea of people shouted, 'AMEN!'

Reinhard was like a doctor in the spirit. He took authority over the devil's work and bound him in EVERY area. Then he promptly released God's Word and promises into the atmosphere, allowing the people to take hold of God's truth. What we then witnessed was magnificent. *MIRACLES* began to break out all over the place. Eruptions of praise broke out in pockets of the crowd. Wheelchairs were thrown into the air and passed across the crowd as people regained strength in their limbs. Blind eyes opened. Deaf ears popped open. It was amazing! God was moving, healing, saving, changing lives. Young and old were being touched by the presence and power of the Holy Spirit! At the end of the evening Reinhard prayed for the people to be baptised in the Holy Spirit. He read the scripture below:

> *"Ye shall receive power, after that the Holy Ghost is come upon you; and ye shall be witnesses unto me."*
>
> **Acts 1:8 (KJV)**

After he had read these words and prayed, the Holy Spirit fell on the people and they were instantly baptised in the Spirit. The sound I heard was like Niagara Falls as the crowd shouted and sang to God in their heavenly language. It was absolutely breathtaking!

My life had been shaken and changed during my time in Nigeria. My eyes had witnessed things there that I will never forget. I might be wrong, but I believe that much of the western world has no idea what God is doing in Africa. We hear a lot of bad news about poverty, sickness, war and need and, yes, that's a reality. *BUT,* God is moving on such a grand scale in Africa that it's mind-blowing. I encourage you, if you have the opportunity to go there and witness it first hand, it will short-circuit your mind!

When I returned back to the UK I did my best to communicate to our worship team what I had seen and heard but I could not do it justice at all. However, the fire that raged in my soul burned brighter than ever before and I began to think in my heart, if God can do it in Africa, then why not the United Kingdom? Could it be that God could move on that kind of scale in my country? If it were the case, we would have the UK saved in no time! Oh for the day when we begin to see stadiums filled with people praising and loving God on a regular basis! I'm aware it's happening in seed form at the moment, but I'm believing that I am going to be a part of the generation that sees this every weekend! You may be thinking, 'Hmm, nice thought, Mark, and it's great that you're excited.'

But friend, when you've seen it with your own eyes it does something to you. When you bump into a living reality of what God is able to do through someone, you begin to ask yourself the question, 'Could God use me in that way, too?' I believe the answer is YES. YES HE COULD!

The presence of the Holy Spirit is not weak, He is STRONG! His eyes run to and fro across the whole earth in order to show Himself strong on behalf of those whose hearts are loyal to Him. He will use a faith-filled person powerfully. He will use a devoted person in a magnificent way. He will use a dependable and dedicated person in an extraordinary way. And He will use a trustworthy person in a way that surpasses those who live a mediocre life. He is looking at your life right at this moment and He is saying. *'I am ready to move on your behalf, I am always multiple steps ahead of you. I am more than ready to act upon My Word on your behalf! I am the same Holy Spirit who walked with Christ. My power has not decreased and My will has not changed. I wait for those who wholeheartedly believe My Word. I am then free to confirm the Word with signs following. Are you ready? I AM. Are you up for it? I AM. Do you wholeheartedly believe My Word? Yes? THEN LET'S GO FOR IT!'*

CHAPTER 7

RESTORER OF GOD'S PRESENCE

s a follower of Jesus Christ I am aware that I am a restorer of God's presence, a bringer of heaven. Wherever I go, He goes. Greater is Christ within me than any other opposing force in this world!

My calling and responsibility is to diffuse the fragrance of God's love and grace to a world that desperately needs it. Therefore I must be ready and alert in every season to give away the precious hope that is within me. There is unquestionably so much brokenness in this world and as a believer I realise that I have the resources available to me that will help bring healing and restoration. Yes, I am a restorer of God's presence!

RESTORING THE ARK OF GOD

It's no surprise to me that during the exact time King David was restoring the presence of God back into the centre of Israel's worship experience that he was confronted behind closed doors about his conduct.

After this great moment in Bible history (2 Samuel 6), Scripture records that David returned to his own house to celebrate what had just taken place and to bring blessing to his family. However, when he walked through his front door his wife Michal came out to speak to him and unfortunately she didn't have a good word to say about the day he had just experienced. In fact Michal was probably not aware of it at the time but what she had to say to her husband was a direct assault from the enemy. But let me get back to that in a little while. I want to spend a little bit of time painting a picture of the events that led up to that moment in time.

David understood deeply that the presence of God was the very thing that separated and distinguished Israel from any other nation on the earth. Without it Israel would be sunk! They would be just like any other godless people. When David entered his season of kingly rule, the Ark of the Covenant, which represented the presence of God, had been in captivity with Israel's enemies for twenty years, and this weighed heavily upon his heart. God's presence meant everything to him. He knew that he could not reign as king without it. David knew from whom his success would come. He understood that his victory, strength and supply were in God and not in man, neither were they in his earthly abilities. He needed to restore the presence of God to have dominion over his enemies and he needed the presence of God to have continued success.

David's first attempt to restore the Ark failed because of the way in which the approach was handled. The Bible tells us in 2 Samuel 6 that the cart which was bearing the Ark hit a pothole, and David's friend Uzzah put out his hand to stop it from falling. We are told that God's anger was aroused against him. God took Uzzah's life for his irreverent act. Uzzah was judged because he reached out in haste not realising he was touching the holiest thing on the planet!

After the death of Uzzah the Bible tells us that David was angry with God, which I find interesting because it wasn't really David's place to become angry with God. What David would later find out was that there was a way in which the Ark of the Covenant needed to be carried and handled. God is a God of detail and He likes things done in a particular way. The right approach equals the right results. David's anger soon turned to fear and then the fear drew him into a deeper conversation with himself. He said in himself, 'How then can the Ark of God come to me?' What a great question to ask. I think it's a question we need to ask ourselves, 'How can I experience more of God?'

LET'S TRY THAT AGAIN!

We can see in 2 Samuel 6 that David's second attempt in restoring the Ark was completely different to the first. He had three months to think about it. We read that the Ark was brought up into the city this time with *gladness*, *sacrifice*, *praise*, *dancing* and *celebration*! Every time those who were carrying the Ark took six steps, oxen and fatted sheep were sacrificed to God. David didn't want to get anything wrong this time!

I notice that in the second approach *gladness* is mentioned first.

We go through many trials, heartaches and setbacks in this life and, because of this, we ask God for help, and rightly so. God is merciful, gracious, kind and willing to help us in our time of need. God understands the times and seasons in our world. He knows exactly what we are facing and what we're going through. There is a season to mourn. *BUT* we need to understand when it's time to get up, dust ourselves off and move into a season of *gladness*. And if that means being *glad* ahead of time in order to get our breakthrough then that's what we need to do!

Let me encourage you, friend – the way you're going to find your breakthrough and your next blessing is by being *glad ahead of time* and, by doing so, you're going to unlock something from within the heart of God into your situation. He's going to call the angels over and say, 'Hey, look at my kids! They're in a mess and they're still being glad anyway! I need to bless them right now!' Being glad ahead of time is an act of faith. It's saying, 'God, Your Word is the truth and I'm going to believe Your Word above the current situation I'm going through!'

The second thing that is mentioned in David's restoration of the Ark is *sacrifice*.

Sacrifice is an essential quality that unearths more of God's presence in our lives. God is attracted to sacrifice. It is well pleasing to Him. Now sacrifice and giving are one and the same thing, they are intrinsically linked. We can see that David was extravagant in his sacrifice, he wasn't concerned about the cost. What he was concerned about was doing things in the right way. Every time those carrying the Ark took six steps, a sacrifice took place. Wow! Every six steps! This speaks to me and reminds me that I need to be doing the same if I want to continue to see God show up in my life. I am compelled to walk out a life of sacrifice because it's well pleasing to Him.

I have come to understand on many occasions that God's over-arching plan for my life is much more valuable than some of the things I have planned for myself. Therefore I have learned to sacrificially give my plans over to God because He knows me better than I know myself. When we do this for God what we get in return is always so much greater. Sometimes that return may not look like the best road to take. It may not be filled with stage lights, wads of cash or the idea of success that you first sought, but it will be filled with the priceless treasure of God's kiss on your life. And it's that that I seek!

The greater the purpose, the greater the pain; the greater the crown, the greater the cross

The Bible tells us in Hebrews 12:2,

> *"For the joy that was set before [Jesus] endured the cross, despising the shame, and has sat down at the right hand of the throne of God."*

For *the joy* that was set before Him He *sacrificed* His life! And that joy, my friend, was for your and my redemption! It was a tangible joy! It was the joy of billions of souls being reconciled into a relationship with their Creator. Extraordinary! When Jesus hung upon the cross and laid down His life He knew that His payoff was close at hand, that's what spurred Him on. Nobody else saw the payoff. But He did! He had it firmly fixed in His heart. He was going to get His hands on the joy. It's so much easier to go through sacrifice with the hope of an outcome or a tangible joy! Believe me, that's why it's vital to have a hope of some kind set in your heart. Life can be incredibly tough at times. But in saying that, I believe that God would never ask you to sacrifice anything in your world unless there was something so much better ahead of you.

GET YOUR DANCE ON!

We're told that King David *danced* with all his might. I would have loved to see that! Maybe if I ask him in heaven he might show me a few moves? I wonder if he would've given Justin Timberlake a run for his money? Ha! As David ushered in God's presence, I can imagine him dancing with a sense of abandonment and childlike freedom, not at all mindful of those around him. The Bible tells us that he removed his kingly robes and danced in his under garments. He must have danced up a sweat! He was really going for it! Awesome.

The undergarment he danced in was called an ephod. Now an ephod was usually worn by a priest whose responsibility was to offer up sacrifices towards God on behalf of the people. This gives us an insight into David's priestly office. However, in this instance he was offering sacrifices towards God on behalf of Israel so the presence of God could be ushered in for *all* of Israel to enjoy! Much the same as what Christ did on the cross when He offered Himself up as a perfect sacrifice. Christ was responsible for ushering in the New Covenant and the promise of the Holy Spirit. God dwelling within man! Hallelujah!

There was a great celebration happening on that day and I believe this is what God's church should be like. We have a victory to celebrate! Whether we feel like it or not, feelings don't change the reality of what Jesus has accomplished for us. We have a Victor! David *danced, rejoiced, shouted* and *celebrated*! I believe he was modelling the kind of atmosphere and lifestyle that he wanted the nation under his leadership to enjoy and imitate. His dance was a prophetic proclamation of triumph and joy! He was breaking the back of religious pomp and ceremony! He was breaking the back of depression and heaviness! He was breaking the back of his enemies by letting them know that his God was with him! I'm getting excited as I write this and I can feel the power of God stirring in my heart! Wow!

During the celebration the Bible tells us that king David began *distributing gifts* to the people. He not only had prepared himself to give to God but he had also prepared himself to give to the people he led. They all went away blessed from the experience. This should be our heart's cry too. We are blessed to be a blessing. We are conduits of God that pass on heaven's resources to the world. We cannot and should not hold God's blessings to ourselves. We are compelled by the Holy Spirit to pass them on! Let's have hearts that give like David.

Now, as I said at the beginning of this chapter, David went home with the intention of blessing his family with the same excitement and extravagant atmosphere that he had experienced that day. But unfortunately he was not greeted with the same level of excitement, to say the least. I'm sorry to burst your excitement bubble here but I'd love for you to read these next few scriptures with me because I think there's something we can learn.

> *"Now as the ark of the LORD came into the City of David, Michal, Saul's daughter, looked through a window and saw King David leaping and whirling before the LORD; and she despised him in her heart."*

> *"Then David returned to bless his household. And Michal the daughter of Saul came out to meet David, and said, 'How glorious was the king of Israel today, uncovering himself today in the eyes of the maids of his servants, as one of the base fellows shamelessly uncovers himself!' So David said to Michal, 'It was before the LORD, who chose me instead of your father and all his house, to appoint me ruler over the people of the LORD, over Israel. Therefore I will play music before the LORD. And I will be even more undignified than this, and will be humble in my own sight. But as for the*

maidservants of whom you have spoken, by them I will be held in honour.' Therefore Michal the daughter of Saul had no children to the day of her death."

Samuel 6:16, 20-23

Wow! I don't think you could really get two more opposing contrasts of opinion regarding what had just taken place. On one hand we can see that David and his maidservants were in high spirits because of this incredible moment. The restoration of the Ark was taking place! Yet we can see that Michal was on a completely different planet mentally and emotionally. The Bible says, 'she despised him in her heart' (2 Samuel 6:16).

What was going on with Michal? What was she thinking? What was happening inside of her to cause her to react that way? Well, let's dig a little deeper and take a look at her and David's conversation because I believe God allowed us to hear it for a reason. I think there are some key thoughts here that we can lift out which will help us as believers if we're ever confronted with the same thing.

Firstly, we need to understand that Michal was the daughter of Israel's previous king, Saul. Now, just that statement should cause us to think about her in a different way. Saul spent much of his reign as king trying to destroy David and on this occasion Michal seemed to carry the same mindset.

We all know how powerful the atmosphere of a home can be and how much this can affect someone by stealth. I wonder what Michal's home was like as a girl? If Saul's character is anything to measure this by, I believe she grew up in a home that was full of insecurity, control, jealousy, opinion and criticism, as these were prominent character traits of her father that were expressed on many occasions. We can see that these traits were also woven into the fabric of who Michal presented herself to be in this passage of scripture.

2 Samuel 6:20 tells us that David returned to his own house with the intention of blessing it, but how quickly the tables were turned on him. I really feel for David because he had gone through so much already. He had experienced years of Saul hunting him down like a fugitive and now he stood in front of Saul's daughter, his wife who had the intention of controlling him and keeping him small.

Michal didn't have a good word to say to David about the amazing day he had just experienced. All she did was seek to tame him because of her insecurity. I say 'insecurity' because Michal was obviously extremely uncomfortable about the way David had conducted himself. I believe she had *no frame of reference* to compare his behaviour to. It was a way she wasn't used to and a way she didn't understand. I believe she had no ability to connect with the moment David had been caught up in (when he danced with all of his might) because that level of joy and rejoicing were unfamiliar to her, therefore it looked stupid and foreign. Maybe as a little girl Michal had experienced joy on this level but had that been stifled and trodden on? There are many homes like this; maybe you've experienced an atmosphere where there was a void of joy and happiness. In this instance, when insecurity took hold of Michal, it instantly created a critical spirit which began to manifest itself in a controlling manner. The reality is, *what you don't understand you'll try to tidy up and control.* 'She despised David in her heart.' Wow, those are very strong words and it was a horrible opinion to have.

This really bothers me because, sadly, I have hit up against this kind of critical spirit in the church. Most of the time it comes from people who have been a Christian for a long time and think they know better. But, if the truth be told, they have lost their passion for Jesus and have lost their joy and sense of fun. They've forgotten what it feels like to be alive and free! They would say they're being 'mature', but I believe being mature is being able to *read a moment* and to know what it requires. The Psalms constantly provoke God's people to lift up a shout unto God and to rejoice! Well, bless God, I'm going to do what it says! Amen! I'm not going to be dominated by 'Mr or Mrs I've-been-sucking-on-lemons-all-day!'

As believers in Jesus Christ there is a sound that we are called to emulate and that's the *sound of heaven*. It's a different sound to the sound of the earth and is tapped into by our hearts not our heads. It's a victorious and powerful sound. It's the sound of joy and freedom and it demands a response. I believe David was hearing this sound that day and his behaviour was his response.

DAVID'S RESPONSE TO MICHAL

David's reply to Michal was spot on. I believe this is the kind of response we need to have (and remember, David is dealing with the line of thought Michal is yielding to). Firstly he said, 'It was before the LORD.' He instantly dealt with man's opinion. He wasn't doing what he did to please man in any way. His desire was to please God. That's such a key for us – simple, yet so profound. I don't know about you but I've spent too much of my life trying to please *people* and it wore me out! People can be so fickle. They are cool with you acting like you act one day and then the next day they completely change their mind. Life's too short to try to fit in with what pleases people. I mean, don't get me wrong, I love and respect people, but this is a different issue. David knew in his heart that he was being manipulated and controlled, and he had to do something about it.

The second thing David addressed was Michal's inability to flow with him as God's man. He said to her, 'It was before the LORD, who chose *me* instead of your father and all his house, to appoint me ruler over the people of the LORD, over Israel.'

David was saying, (paraphrased) 'Hey babe, there's a new leader in town and now you need to align yourself with him, and if that doesn't fit with you it's not going to go well with you. Your father is no longer on the throne, I am; and I have a way of getting things done. This is how I roll. If that upsets you, Michal, then you need to get over it.'

And lastly he said (paraphrased), 'If you think what I did

today was bad, then you ain't seen nothing yet! I will become even more undignified than this!'

David was trying to help Michal understand that this was just the beginning! 'I've been flowing like this for a long time and it's working for me. This is actually how I got from where I was to where I am today – from shepherding my Dad's sheep to shepherding God's people; from a kid to a king. And if you try to dull me down or tame this part of me, you're going to get burned. You've gotta let the lion that's inside of me *ROAR*! I have a God to praise. He has done so many good things in my life and I can't be silent! There's a new king in town and this is how the new king operates! He's a praiser. He's a worshipper! He's a mighty man of war!'

The incredibly sad thing was that God judged Michal's critical heart and she became barren, not being able to conceive David's children.

I believe this is what happens to people who despise and criticise what God is doing through someone – they become unfruitful as a person and they are not able to conceive on another level. Their productivity is halted. God forbid that it ever happens to us.

A PRETTY FULL ON CHAPTER, DON'T YOU THINK?

My prayer is that you would have a spirit like David and be free in your love and devotion towards God. If you are going through a time of struggle and adversity, I pray that you would set your face like flint and be true to the way God has wired you as a person. Be free in your heart, friend, and be free in your mind. Don't allow critical and negative opinions to poison your heart. Be secure in how God has made you to be. Don't allow anyone to change the part of you that God loves. You, like David, are a restorer of God's presence and need to remain free in your heart to allow His presence to be released. David knew himself well and was completely secure in how he rolled as a person. We must be the same. The fact is, the enemy wants to slow you down by putting roadblocks in your way. He wants to stop the flow of God's river in your heart by creating dams or contrary opinions. Restorers of God's presence know how to break through barriers and transcend their environment. They know how to rise above the tide. And the way they do it is by being *strong in the LORD and secure in themselves!* Be glad, friend. Be sacrificial. Be full of joy and rejoice in His presence. Enjoy your life! And be the *RESTORER* God has called you to be. Amen.

CHAPTER 8

FILLED WITH FRAGRANCE

"And being in Bethany at the house of Simon the leper, as He sat at the table, a woman came having an alabaster flask of very costly oil of spikenard. Then she broke the flask and poured it on His head. But there were some who were indignant among themselves, and said, 'Why was this fragrant oil wasted? For it might have been sold for more than three hundred denarii and given to the poor.' And they criticised her sharply. But Jesus said, 'Let her alone. Why do you trouble her? She has done a good work for Me. For you have the poor with you always, and whenever you wish you may do them good; but Me you do not have always. She has done what she could. She has come beforehand to anoint My body for burial. Assuredly, I say to you, wherever this gospel is preached in the whole world, what this woman has done will also be told as a memorial to her.'"

Mark 14:3-9

*O*ver the years I have been impacted in many different ways by this passage of scripture. It's an incredible story that opens up the door on the house of Simon the leper, a man who, only a few chapters before, is miraculously healed by Jesus. It also captures a priceless moment in time, one of Mary's heartfelt worship of Jesus and her costly sacrifice. In addition to this, it hands us insight into the forces that seek to fight against us giving God our very best in worship, factors that create resistance and tension. It also helps us understand that there will always be circumstances that press against us, seeking to choke our song of praise and adoration to our King.

I love placing myself in this story as a bystander. It helps the story come alive to me. I find that I can get a fuller picture of what was going on. So, if you don't mind, as I write a few thoughts down, please allow me to take a few liberties.

There's only mention of one woman in this story, so we are entering a very male dominated room which I can imagine to be noisy and hearty, a room that's filled with conversation, where the smell of freshly cooked food and freshly poured wine are in the air. We are at Simon the leper's home. He is a Pharisee, an extremely religious man, so I can imagine that some of the conversation is weighty and intense, filled with questions about morality and spirituality.

On the other side of the room there's laughter from a few of the disciples who are telling far-fetched stories of fishing escapades. I can also hear a quiet business conversation coming from Judas, based around money and making lots of it.

Then there's the unspoken conversation that springs from a deeper place in the heart of a man. It's a conversation based around comparison and position and titles. It's the silent conversation a man has with himself about his own value. Does he measure up? Is he good enough to be in this company? He bases his own 'self-importance', or on the flip-side of that, his own 'self-sabotage' around his achievements and in his ability to climb to the top of the ladder.

You see, a man likes to have a handle on things. He likes to be in charge or in control, it makes him feel centred and at ease. Men thrive on the knowledge of being self-sufficient and of being a success. It makes him feel powerful. It makes him feel worth something. It makes him feel like a man. But then again, on the downside, when a man feels like he's a failure or not good enough, he'll go underground, go subterranean, even in a crowded room. Inwardly he'll begin to pick himself apart.

This is the kind of conversation that Jesus had the ability to hear: the unspoken. He is the reader of people's hearts, of their motives and intentions. This is what made people vulnerable and uneasy around Him at times.

The Bible tells us that Jesus would not entrust Himself to man because He knew what was in them. No doubt on this occasion He had a grip on the elements that filled the room.

It's at this moment the atmosphere changes from a dinner party into a heartfelt worship service.

As everyone takes their seats and begins to eat there's a

knock at Simon's front door. Simon looks embarrassed and hastily looks around the table to be confident that all his guests are present. Yes, everyone who has an invitation is there. The look on his face quickly changes from one of embarrassment to impatience and frustration. He then proceeds to excuse himself from the table, asking one of his servants to answer the door and send away whoever it is. He returns to the table and apologises to Jesus and his guests. Jesus just smiles and continues to eat his meal.

Suddenly a small commotion breaks out as a woman bursts through the front door carrying something under her arm. She's talking quite loudly exclaiming, 'I must see the Master. I have something for Him. He's here, right? I must see him.'

Simon's servant tries to grab the woman as she quickly walks up the hallway towards the dining room. The servant shouts after her, 'Um, excuse me, where do you think you're going? Excuse me, you can't go in there!'

Too late – the woman enters the dining room. Stepping through the door she hastily looks around for Jesus. Her breathing is nervously heavy. Her eyes are filled with tears and her face is filled with a mixture of expressions written all over it: desperation; sorrow; apology; a hint of gladness; love, hope, it's all there. Suddenly her eyes lock with Jesus' eyes. Her expression then changes to one of elated joy. She becomes still and time freezes. Her heart races and a feeling of incredible warmth, acceptance and safety rushes over her body, emanating from the inside out.

While this is taking place Simon quickly stands to his feet, as do some of the disciples. Everyone looks embarrassed for Simon and also for the woman. Simon raises his arms and quickly addresses the situation. He tries to have one of his servants escort the woman out of his home but Jesus places a firm hand on Simon's arm as if to say, 'Leave her alone.' Simon is shocked by Jesus' response and hastily turns towards Him but then freezes as He sees His face. Jesus' eyes are ablaze; they are sure and strong. Yet there is still a peace that radiates from His being. Simon the leper then nods to his servants and asks them to leave her alone. He stays standing. The disciples again take their seats. Jesus is not at all moved. He has stayed in His seat the whole time.

Before another word is spoken the woman walks towards Jesus and time stands still. Glancing towards the other men she seems to inwardly lose her balance, but then quickly locking eyes with Jesus again she finds her inner strength. As she nears where He is sitting she drops to her knees and takes from under her arm a bag that she has been carrying. There are a few uneasy coughs from the men but the woman is not distracted by them this time and continues to prepare her small ceremony. Reaching into her bag she pulls from it something familiar to those in the room. It's a small container that holds within it some of the most costly perfume money can buy: spikenard. There are confused looks from Simon's guests because people use this kind of perfume to prepare the dead for burial. Little did they know that God was using this woman to prophetically prepare His Son for His soon-coming burial.

The woman then lifts her hands with the flask full of spikenard and swiftly breaks it on the hard floor next to her. She then proceeds to stand up and empty its delicate and costly contents upon the head of Jesus. The wonderful fragrance begins to permeate the room filling it with the most incredible aroma. It's at this moment the atmosphere changes from a dinner party into a heartfelt worship service. As the flask is emptied the woman begins to openly weep. During this moment she has forgotten about those who surround her. She only has eyes for One. She falls to her knees, kissing the feet of Jesus, wiping her tears from His feet with her hair.

As this is taking place Simon the leper begins to realise who this woman is. She's a woman with a reputation, with a sordid past. Yes, he knows exactly who she is! Simon inwardly begins to judge and criticise her, thinking, 'If Jesus were a prophet He would know what kind of woman this is; she's a sinner!'

The atmosphere is harshly broken by the voice of Judas who loudly expresses his opinion, 'Lord, this is such a waste! We could've sold this flask of spikenard for three hundred silver pieces and used the money to help the poor!' A few of the men become indignant and openly agree with Judas, causing the atmosphere to become angry and intense. The woman becomes frightened.

In the midst of this commotion Jesus stands up with kingly authority! There's a burning fire in His eyes. INSTANTLY the room becomes silent. He glares at everyone for what seems like an eternity. His eyes then fall towards the woman knelt before Him. Jesus briefly smiles at her with pity and compassion. She stares back at Him now trembling with fear, but the look on His face calms her down a little. She knows He is on her side.

Jesus looks towards Judas. Judas becomes uneasy and shifts in his seat. Jesus says, 'Leave this woman alone! Why are you giving her a hard time? She has just done something wonderfully significant for Me. You will have the poor with you every day for the rest of your lives. Whenever you feel like it, you can do something for them. But not so with Me. She did what she could when she could – she pre-anointed My body for burial. And you can be sure that wherever in the whole world the gospel is preached, what she just did is going to be talked about admiringly.'

There is complete silence in the room.

Jesus then turns towards Simon and says, 'Simon, I have something to teach you.'

Simon responds quickly, 'Teacher, say it.'

Jesus continues: 'There was a certain lender who had two people who owed him money. One owed five hundred silver pieces and the other fifty. And when they had nothing with which to repay him, he forgave them both. Tell Me, which one will love him more?'

Simon replied, 'I guess the one who owed him more.'

And He said to him, 'That's right.'

Then Jesus turned to the woman and said to Simon, 'Do you see this woman? I entered your house; but you gave Me no water for My feet, but she has washed My feet with her tears and wiped them with her hair. You gave Me no kiss but this woman has not ceased to kiss My feet since the time she came in. You did not anoint My head but this woman has anointed My head with fragrant oil. Therefore I say to you, her sins, which are many, are forgiven, for she loved much. But those who are forgiven little, love little.'

Then Jesus said to her, 'Your sins are forgiven.'

There were whispers at the table as the men reasoned among themselves, saying things like, 'Who is this that He even forgives sins?'

Then Jesus said to the woman, 'Your faith has saved you. Go in peace.'

Gathering her things, the woman quickly rose to her feet and left the room. She was gone. The men were left alone. But the smell of fragrant oil was still lingering in the air. The residue of tender heartfelt worship still filled the room. Nobody knew what to do and what to say. There was an awkwardness amongst the men; they were speechless.

Let me say just a few words about this passage of scripture that I believe will help you as a worshipper of Jesus Christ.

There will always be a battle on for your breakthrough in worship. The enemy is the accuser of the brethren and has a plan and strategy to keep you out of the richest and most intimate places with Jesus and only your willingness to allow your worship to 'cost you' will bring you into those rich and wonderful places. This woman pushed past criticism and the resistance she felt and kept moving towards Jesus, bringing her costly sacrifice with her. She then broke the container that held its contents, meaning she had no way to use again the precious fragrance she had poured out. She wanted to give all to Jesus and not keep anything back for herself.

This speaks to me of complete abandonment and sincere trust in the One she was worshipping. She was declaring in this experience her understanding that God was her source and supply; that God was the One who could forgive and restore; that God was the one who could mend her brokenness. Praise God! She fell right at His feet. She didn't fall at the feet of her circumstances. She didn't fall at the feet of another person who could only supply a fraction of the answer she was looking for. She came to Jesus, the Author and Finisher of her faith, the One who had the power to erase the pages of her past, place a pen in her hand with grace-filled ink so she was able to write a brand new story.

I love that Jesus said to Simon regarding the woman that, 'Those who are forgiven of much, love much.' I can definitely relate to this because I, too, was forgiven of many mistakes. There are things in my past that I have chosen to forget that are dead and buried in the graveyard of forgiveness, things that I will ever be thankful to Jesus for paying the price for. Former mistakes now forgiven that have become the catalyst in digging the deep well of love and thankfulness I now daily express to my precious Jesus in worship.

This woman did not care about the cost of what she poured

out because she knew that what she would receive from Jesus would be worth so much more: forgiveness, affirmation, unconditional love, strength, a second chance to live the God kind of life that she was always destined for. She understood that money could not fix her problem. No, only an encounter with Jesus could fix it. And she knew that if she could go through this process of worship and sacrifice, her life would never ever be the same again!

She filled the room with the fragrance of her love for Jesus. And that fragrance not only influenced the room she was in but it also escaped the room and impacted future generations from that time on. Her costly worship left a mark on history.

May we always let our worship of Jesus Christ cost us something, for it is in the cost that God gives back. It's in the cost that a harvest of righteousness is born. It's in the cost that you receive something from the heart of God that the world could never give you. May our worship release the kind of fragrance that affects everyone around us. May it permeate the atmosphere and put to flight any form of resistance the enemy could throw our way. And may our worship be centred on Christ and Christ alone.

NOTE

In the last two chapters of this book I want to change direction a little and encourage those who are dealing with adversity or negotiating major changes in their lives. These are two things that I have recently journeyed through myself.

It was wonderful for me to know that I could call upon God for comfort and courage when I was confronting challenges. And it is also wonderful to know that during transition and change God was there to help me negotiate a new road. The Bible says in Proverbs 16:9,

"A man's heart plans his way, but the LORD directs his steps."

I found this to be so true. We can have all the plans in the world, and that's a good thing, but at times we need a word from heaven to help guide us and bring clarity. I found there were definite times in my life where God would step in and bring solid direction. I'm so thankful for that as I probably would've made a mess of things. I came to realise deeply that God is not only the God of yesterday and forever, but He is the God of my today. He is the God of my right now.

So, as you read on, friend, I pray that these last two chapters would continue to be strength for your road.

CHAPTER 9

FINDING COURAGE IN TOUGH TIMES

At times our lives can be challenged with many different circumstances that, more often than not, present themselves unexpectedly, so it's vital that we are able to find *courage* within. Life can change on a dime and what you once thought you could find refuge in can overnight fall into the sea. Therefore we need to have our lives anchored into God and God alone. When push comes to shove, and the friends that you thought were friends leave you, don't call you anymore and begin to speak ill of you, or the job that you thought you would have for the rest of your life suddenly disappears through redundancy, or a loved one suddenly becomes sick and in need of constant support, you need to be able to find something in the bank of your soul that will cause you to get back on your feet again. You need to be like King David in the Bible who *encouraged himself in the Lord* so he was able to withstand the frontal assault of the enemy. The courage that David found in God caused him to regain his strength again and push through the resistance he felt.

In this chapter I want to encourage you, friend, to be *vigilant* in taking quality time out to *strengthen* yourself in God, particularly if you're called to any form of leadership. I have found that more often than not the leader is the one who gets hit by strong challenges first. They are the ones who are positioned at the front of their church, team, business or family and are leading the charge. Therefore, the enemy knows that if he can take them down, he can affect those they influence. The enemy's crafty, too. He's well aware that if he *can't* take the leader down he'll go after the people that are most precious to them.

Let's read a few scriptures from the Bible that will serve as a foundation for the things I want to share with you in this chapter.

> *"Now David was greatly distressed, for the people spoke of stoning him, because the soul of all the people was grieved, every man for his sons and his daughters. But David strengthened [encouraged] himself in the LORD his God. Then David said to Abiathar the priest, Ahimelech's son, 'Please bring the ephod here to me.' And Abiathar brought the ephod to David. So David inquired of the LORD, saying, 'Shall I pursue this troop? Shall I overtake them?' And He answered him, 'Pursue, for you shall surely overtake them and without fail recover all.'"*
>
> **1 Samuel 30:6-8**

Giving context to this passage of scripture, this was one of the darkest moments in David's life. Ziklag, the town in which David, his family, his troops and their families were staying had been burned with fire. The enemy had not only plundered David and his troops' camp, but had also taken their wives and children. As you can imagine there was deep sorrow and distress in their souls at that time, so much so that David's men thought of stoning him. They actually thought of killing their leader! This was a tough day at the office for David to say the least. I've experienced tough days, and no doubt you have, too, but this causes my tough days to pale into insignificance!

As I've read the words in this chapter I've wondered at times what must have been going through David's troops' minds that day. I mean, how did they arrive at a decision to stone their leader? What were his troops saying? Maybe it went something like this:

'This is what we get in return for devoting our lives to David, the loss of our families and our loved ones? We have given our lives to follow him and serve him, yet all we seem to get in return is resistance and heartache!'

'Is following him really worth it anymore? We seem to be getting further away from the hope and promise of a better life. Maybe we've been chasing a fantasy? He's leading all of us into loss and destruction!'

'Look, we've lost everything: our wives, our children! Enough is enough! We need to stone him – yes, we need to kill him!'

The Bible says that David was *greatly distressed*. I don't blame him! Now hopefully this is not something that we will ever have to face, but I think you'll agree with me that there are seasons in our lives where we feel *overwhelmed* in many other ways.

Maybe right now you feel like you've got challenges on every side and things are closing in around you. You feel stuck and can't see a way out. Maybe you've lost your job and you're not sure how you're going to pay your bills this month. Or you're experiencing incredible pressure in your church ministry and you seem to be going around and around in circles and nothing's changing.

Well, let me say this, friend: I think David's response to the mess he was confronted with was incredible. I think we can learn from him and be totally inspired. Let's find out how he handled this situation and what his response was.

> "But David **encouraged** and strengthened himself in
> the Lord his God."
>
> 1 Samuel 30:6 (AMP, emphasis mine)

In his darkest moment David sought God for courage and strength. He drew away from the crowd. He drew away from people's heartache and anger and went on the lookout for some kind of answer to the mess that surrounded him. *David went to seek the Lord.*

I think the idea of drawing away in moments like these is so important for us. You have to train your soul to find an uncontaminated place where you can again find heaven's perspective on things.

You see, when your back is against the wall and there is nowhere left to go, you've got to know where to look and who to look to. You've got to get desperate. You've got to find something within your soul that causes you to fall on God. David was in a position where all he had was seemingly lost. He was in limbo with *nothing* and *no one* to rely on: no family, no friends, no things, *only God.* Have you ever been there, friend?

It was in that place that David needed to realise that God was enough

David knew full well where his courage and strength would come from. It would not come from his status, nor would it come from man. It would not come from his bank account and it would definitely not come from his circumstances. He understood that if he could *hear from God* he could deal with the fallout and confusion. He understood that if he could hear God speak he would know exactly what to do and how to deal with this mess.

In my mind's eye I can see David in desperation worshipping God that day, remembering His precious promises, reminding himself of the many breakthroughs and good things that He had done in his world. Bringing to mind the promise that God was going to bring him into the fullness of a kingdom that he would rule and reign, which he had not yet possessed.

It's great to remind ourselves, isn't it? Remembering the times when we had nothing and God provided something at the eleventh hour. Remembering how God healed someone we love. Remembering the time when we were at our wits' end our answer came through and the storm was stilled. Remembering how God protected us from death and destruction when we could have lost our lives like some of the people we used to hang out with. David encouraged himself in the Lord. Not the arm of the flesh, no, not in man, but in the King of kings and the Lord of lords!

I can see David on his face before God in anguish and bitterness of soul. Yet he had come to the right place. David positioned himself to worship and inquire of the Lord. I can see David worshipping and praising God in utter abandonment. I mean, this was the God who took him from shepherding the sheep to being a valiant warrior and the promised king over Israel! This was the God who had given him the courage to take down Goliath! And this was the God that had delivered him from countless battles! He deserved David's worship and praise!

I can see David's heart becoming full again: full of strength, full of gratefulness, full of the fuel he needed to win his loved ones back! Full of courage, and full of the presence of God.

David could have moved in haste to run after his enemy and do things in his own strength but he chose not to. Let me encourage you: when things seem to be overwhelming you, the best thing that you can do is *wait on the Lord*. Don't run off and make a half-baked decision. Too many people make this mistake and make things even worse. If David had responded straight away he would not have had God's Word and opinion on the matter and he would not have had any of his six hundred troops on his side. The Bible tells us that *the battle is not ours it is the Lord's.* The worst thing we can do in a crisis is go about fighting things in our own strength. I've realised in many circumstances and trying times that flesh and blood cannot change a thing. I need supernatural intervention to fix things! I need the hand of God to intervene. I need to pray prayers like, 'God, I can't do this without You! Help me! Help me break through! Help me, God, defeat my enemies!' In tough times may we learn to seek the Lord regarding the next step.

> *"Wait on the LORD; be of good courage, and He shall strengthen your heart; wait, I say, on the LORD!"*
>
> **Psalm 27:14**

GOD RESPONDS TO DAVID

It must have been difficult to do, but David forced himself into a position where he could hear God's voice. I mean what did God think about this? He desperately needed some answers. Then, when the timing was right, David asked God a question, 'Lord, should I pursue my enemy?' And God said, 'Yes.' God strengthened David by telling him that without fail he would recover all! He would recover his family, his troops' families and all their stuff! Everything! Well, that's all David needed to hear! He knew that God was going to back him up!

I can just see David with fiery eyes, setting his face like flint and walking back into the presence of those messed up and angry men to announce that they were going to pursue the enemy and win their families back! There was obviously faultless conviction in what he said, because six hundred angry men who were talking about stoning him laid aside their heartache and their issues to follow him and take down the enemy!

During the chase they came to a place called the Brook Besor and two hundred men were not able to go on because of complete exhaustion. But David didn't let this sidetrack him from his mission. He let them rest and continued on with four hundred men. He lost a third of his church that day and still wasn't swayed!

Shortly after that they came across one of the enemy's slaves who informed David and his men where their families were.

The Bible tells us that, after finding the enemy, David and his four hundred men attacked the enemy's vast army from twilight until the evening of the next day. Talk about supernatural energy! Only four hundred of the enemy's troops escaped, fleeing on camels, but the battle was won! David and his men recovered *everything* the enemy had stolen from them. Everything! Their wives, their children, all their stuff and plenty of spoils! And you shall, too, my friend! As you trust in the Lord and hear His voice you will plunder the enemy, too! God WILL turn your situation around!

Much to the dismay of some of David's men, the spoils were shared with those who fought and also those who stayed behind. This shows us what kind of man David was. He understood where his victory came from. Had the Lord not stood beside them and fought for them they would've lost the battle.

FIND YOUR COURAGE!

My friend, *courage* is such a powerful force and such a vital quality of spirit. We need courage to carry us through the adversities and challenges of life. No matter how small or great the task is at hand, we need courage to get the job done. Courage is a get-up-and-go quality of spirit, it isn't something we need if we're going to sit in an armchair and talk about taking this world for Christ! Courage has within it the tenacity to face danger, difficulty, uncertainty and pain without itself being overcome. A heart of courage decides that it won't be deflected from its chosen course of action. It pursues and it wins!

The Bible tells us that,

> *"The kingdom of heaven suffers violence, and the violent take it by force"*
>
> **Matthew 11:12**

There must be a force of courage and of action on the inside of us to press on and break new ground! A lot of people don't understand this. They think God is going to serve their best life up on a plate without any work on their part, but this is a fallacy. Just like David, Joshua, too, was encouraged by God to be strong and very courageous. Why? Because in order for Israel to possess the land they had been promised, they would need to confront some serious giants; therefore they would need strength and courage within. The Saviour of the world, Jesus Christ, also needed courage to face the cross. Paul the Apostle needed courage to face the many toils and snares in his ministry. Joseph needed courage to face rejection and jail. Moses needed to find courage in himself to face Pharaoh and, even more, to lead the people of Israel. And the list goes on and on.

GOD IS GETTING YOU READY FOR THE NEXT SHIFT IN YOUR LIFE!

What David didn't understand was that in his darkest moment, God was creating a massive shift in his life. The crown of kingship was on its way to him in Ziklag.

On his worst day, David was on the edge of stepping into one of the greatest seasons of his life. His eyes couldn't see it at the time because he was focused on the battle but, behind the scenes, God was preparing the next season for him. The curtain was just about to go back and all would be revealed.

Saul, David's father-in-law, and Jonathan, his beloved brother-in-law and friend, had been killed in battle on the same day. This would be another huge emotional blow for David but, even so, a man was on his way to find David, who was partly responsible for the death of Saul, carrying Saul's crown. The crown of kingship was in his hands and it was on its way to David. The crown of kingship was always destined for David. It had been prophesied by Samuel that David would be the king over all of Israel.

To tell you the truth, it blows my mind how God can take our worst day and breathe hope and destiny into it. It amazes me how God can paint something beautiful upon the canvas of our lives when the backdrop is filled with pain and turmoil. And it astounds me how God can take a hopeless situation and turn it into triumph for our sake. It seems to me that God uses challenge and heartache to birth something magnificent. When we are at our weakest He steps in and works all things together for our good. It was now time for David to move forwards into the next stage of the kingly anointing God had placed on his life.

I believe with all my heart that God is getting *you* ready for the next shift in your life and He needs you to have courage right now. I encourage you to not lose heart at this time. Stay focused, friend, set your face like flint and press forward, towards the good things that God has promised you, for they are even at the door. They will surely come to pass! You are just passing through a season; you are not going to stay there. The devil would like you to think that nothing's going to change and that your best days are over but that's a lie from the pit of hell! You are in a shift, my friend. Things are moving and things are going to change. Take heart, hold fast and find courage within. Encourage yourself in the Lord. You're closer than ever to your breakthrough! The crown is on its way! And today could be the day.

CHAPTER 10

I'M NOT LOST, I'M JUST IN TRANSITION

I wanted to finish this book with this particular chapter for a reason. The longer I've been alive the more I realise that life is all about transition and change. Life is a series of seasons and within those seasons we have a lesson to learn. Sometimes we stay within the confines of the same season for longer than we planned because we fail to learn its lesson. So we then go back to the start and are able to graduate once we understand its valuable lesson. Or it may be that we stay in the same season because we are too afraid to let go and move on. I think we become afraid to let go of an old season because we give more credence and power to the season itself, and its definition of who it says we are, than to God and His definition of who *He* says we are. We cling onto roles, titles and badges and tend to find our identity, worth and value in what we 'do' as opposed to finding it in God and in 'our being'.

God understands that there is another *you* inside of you, therefore His concern is to place you in an environment where you can be transformed from caterpillar to butterfly, and not just once, but several times over the course of your lifetime. The Bible declares to us in 2 Corinthians 3:18:

> *"We all, with unveiled face, beholding as in a mirror the glory of the Lord, are being transformed into the same image from glory to glory."*

Wow, that's a beautiful thought, but also a very challenging one. We are being lifted from one realm of glory to another. In order to move from one glory to another glory a transition must take place; there must also be a loss of the old in order to gain the new.

You see, to experience a *resurrection* there must be a death. Not a very nice thought, eh? But to be reborn there must be some kind of death. I am sure that when Jesus was in the belly of hell overcoming death, hell and the grave it wasn't a pretty experience for Him. However, what lay on the other side of His willingness to lose the life that He was familiar with was a glorious life and a glorious victory which would not only affect Him but countless others! I wonder what lies on the other side of your next transition? I wonder what lies on the other side of your willingness to change?

So, the reality, friend, is *change is here to stay* and as we learn to embrace it we will be the ones who continue to succeed and flourish in life. It might not look like it but with each day we are becoming more glorious. And as we look towards Jesus and are impacted by His magnificence we should be changing to become more like Him. God knows who we are and what we are destined to become, and He has a vested interest in placing us inside seasons and situations that will bring to life the real you.

TRANSITION HAS A VOICE AND THOSE WHO ARE CHANGING KNOW ITS SOUND

It's difficult to leave something great for the unknown, but that's exactly what I did. *I had to obey God.* It was especially hard because I didn't really have much of an idea of where I was going, but God had said, 'Go!' So, it was time to forge a new path.

I had spent eleven years at the Abundant Life Church in Bradford, England, serving under the incredible leadership of Pastor Paul and Glenda Scanlon, pouring my heart into local church ministry. I loved it. I loved the people I had had the privilege of working with. God had used me, along with others, to raise up some wonderful young leaders who were now spiritually strong and mature enough to be used by God to lead the charge and in many ways do the same as I had done.

Change isn't easy at the best of times, it can be difficult to negotiate, but change is inevitable, and we cannot and should not stay the same. I don't want to be one of those guys who bumps into a friend twenty years down the track who says to me, 'Hey, Mark, you haven't changed a bit!' God forbid! No, I want them to quickly recognise that I'm not the man I used to be. At times during my transition fear and doubt would whisper into my ear and say, 'Mark, what on earth are you doing? Are you sure you want to leave all this? You're doing the wrong thing, this is a mistake.' But even through my doubts I always arrived at the same conclusion, 'It's time to move on and discover new ground.'

What I learned to understand regarding stepping into a new season, was that I was in extremely good company. God particularly encouraged me from the life of Abram, who was asked by God to do the same thing. God's desire for Abram was to establish a new line of faith in him, so He asked him to move from where he was into the *unknown*.

> *"Get out of your country, from your family, and from your father's house, to a land that I will show you. I will make you a great nation; I will bless you, and make your name great; and you shall be a blessing. I will bless those who bless you, and I will curse him who curses you; and in you all the families of the earth shall be blessed."*
> **Genesis 12:1-3**

The first two words that first stood out to me as I read those scriptures were *'get out'*. Now sometimes 'getting out' can run very smoothly and can seemingly happen overnight, but there are other times when getting out can be complex and messy, and can take a long time. Mine was messy and took a long time! Due to health complications, and a fear of the unknown, my transition took longer than it should have but, praise God, my health is fine now and I'm not afraid anymore! So the *'get out'* began – a little delayed but, nonetheless, it began.

I believe God works like this. He gives us instructions or a benchmark to reach towards and then leaves us to change accordingly and sort out the rest. My father-in-law would often say to me, 'Mark, God won't give you a map, He will give you a compass.' I totally agree with him. God gives us a sense of the bigger picture but then leaves us to take care of the finer details. He provokes us towards change by making us feel uncomfortable and by speaking to us about possibilities that seem way beyond our reach and then God leaves us to make the necessary adjustments. At least that was my experience.

You see, when Jesus walked on the water and the disciples saw Him miraculously defying the laws of gravity, Peter was the only one who asked Him if He could come out onto the water, too. Jesus said one word, 'Come.' In other words, Jesus was saying to Peter that, 'You have the ability to do what I'm doing,' but He didn't tell Peter *how* to do it or *where to step* for a more comfortable experience. No, He simply said, 'Come,' and praise God that's exactly what Peter did! He, too, walked on the water! Now he may have sunk a little bit and got his eyes off Jesus, but he got out of the boat!

When I did finally decide to step out, God was definitely in it, although I had to make the first move. I remember being quite apprehensive at the start of my *'get out'* because I would often become confused, particularly when I would hear messages talking about 'connection' and about 'staying attached' because

I was going through something completely different. I was having ideas that were completely the opposite and I felt like a rebel because of it. At times I thought I had given heed to the wrong voice, but after a day or two the dust would settle and I would find myself feeling the same thing inside, that sense of restriction and of wanting to move on. Then, after a while, I would find myself becoming rebalanced and centred again in my decision to 'get out'.

The second thing that stood out to me in this passage of scripture was God saying to Abram, 'To a land that I will show you.' Now I think we need to realise that Abram had been asked by God to move but had not been shown 'where to' yet. He was asked to create movement in his life but by faith had to create his own pathway out.

Now, a lot of people think they have faith at work in them but I might have to disagree with that. You see faith is not something you need when you can see where you're going. Faith is something you need when you can't see anything at all! Faith is something you need when you are off the map! I don't need faith to go to the store because I know exactly where I'm going. However, I do need faith to go somewhere *new*, especially when I have no idea where that is!

TRANSITION BY COLLECTION

From time to time God will transition you into a new place by sending someone ahead of time to literally *collect* you. This happened to me at Hillsong in Sydney, Australia, when I met my now wife Beth. When Beth arrived it was like my future had come to collect me. And God did a double whammy on me because not only did I fall in love with Beth, but I was also completely impacted by her dad's teaching and ministry. This caused me to move all the way from sunny Sydney to rainy Bradford in England, which was a long swim I can tell you! It had to be a God thing, friend, because who would want to leave the sunny beaches of Sydney for . . . um, I think I should just leave it there.

Anyway, here in Bradford I started a new life in a new church and was newly married. Lots of *new* stuff going on there! So, I didn't just need bags of faith, I needed truck loads! Sometimes I look back and laugh about my twelve-thousand-mile move to the UK, because I think I was too caught up in the clouds with God to really care about any negative implications. I just followed my heart and the rest seemed to take care of itself. I found a job a couple of weeks after I arrived in the UK. I was engaged to be married a year or so after I arrived, and I also landed my dream job working at church soon after that! God takes care of things, friend. I must say, too, that my wife is without doubt the prettiest girl on the planet, so that definitely helped with the transition!

That was a change of location for me with some pretty clear signposts. But that was not the case in Abram's situation in the scriptures we just read and it was not the case for the new season I was about to embark on.

SHIFT YOUR THINKING

Transition requires a *shift of thinking* and also requires a change of philosophy or mental language. When you travel to a new country you have to acquaint yourself with a new language and become familiar with a new culture. That is exactly what I found myself having to do. God had in many ways been preparing me for what was coming next but in other ways I had to learn the language of a new season.

When Moses lived in Egypt as a royal son he talked like an Egyptian and acted like an Egyptian but for where he was about to go, which was into a new season, via the desert and the wilderness, a lot of the things he'd learned in Egypt would no longer serve him; actually many of them would be irrelevant! He had to learn *new skills.* He would no longer have servants drawing water from the well for him, no, he had to find his own water, and in the desert that isn't so easy! He would no longer have the system or social structure around him that he was used to, tending to his every need, no, he was going to have to fend for himself. He was going to have to find God in a whole new way, which would prepare him for where he was going to next.

The reason Moses left Egypt was because he had witnessed an Egyptian taskmaster beating an Israelite slave and something had awoken on the inside of him causing him to protect the Israelite slave. Moses murdered the Egyptian taskmaster but another Israelite slave had seen Moses in the act and had communicated this to Moses. Because of this Moses fled for his life fearing the consequences! When Moses murdered the Egyptian, he wasn't aware of it at that time, but in the near future God was going to use him to *deliver* his kinfolk, Israel. His hasty act of protection was actually attached to a deeper response within him. It was attached to the *call* and *commissioning* of God that he would later discover. It obviously came out all wrong at that point. But down the track Moses would confront the injustice that Egypt had brought upon God's prized possession, Israel, and Moses would lead them out of captivity towards their promised land.

RE-COMMISSIONING

Transitions are times when God changes you in order to *re-commission* you. Moses left Egypt one-way and became a different man whose thinking changed during his time in the desert. He actually got in touch with who he *essentially* was, not the Moses people had previously known, not even the Moses that Moses knew, no, *the Moses that God knew.* And when the time was right God would speak to him about the next season of his life. God removed him from where he was and repositioned him in a place where there were no other voices, *just him and God.* And in that uncontaminated place he met with the God of his fathers, Abraham, Isaac and Jacob.

Some of you think that you need to know Mr Big, or you think that you need to go to the big city to live your dream but that's all nonsense. God knows exactly where you are and can meet you right there. God can make you flourish where you are. The book of Isaiah speaks of Jesus as being 'a root out of dry ground', meaning that God can prosper you in a barren place, a tight place and in a place with seemingly no natural resources at your disposal. It is in the desert that Moses learned to understand that God was His all in all, his personal provider and his deliverer.

God also spoke to me in my time of transition from the lives of two amazing people called Zacharias and Elizabeth (Luke, chapters 1 and 2). They were the mother and father of John the Baptist, a fire-and-brimstone preacher who paved the way for the arrival of Jesus Christ.

In Luke chapter 1 we read that Zacharias and Elizabeth had been hoping for a child for many years but were old and had not seen the fulfilment of their desire. You might be in the same position. You may have been believing for your miracle, breakthrough or answer for a long time. Well, let me encourage you: you are in good company. And the great thing is, Zacharias and Elizabeth eventually saw the fulfilment of their desire!

Zacharias was going through the normal, mundane activities of life – the last thing he expected was for an angel of the Lord to suddenly appear to him! A visitation came. It was the angel Gabriel who announced that he and his wife would have a son. The angel was specific about his name, too. He said, 'You should call his name John.'

Zacharias was obviously shocked and taken aback by the experience and proceeded to ask the angel 'How would this happen?' Remember, he was old and so was his wife. He was probably thinking, 'Man, this is going to take a major miracle. My wife is way past the age of child bearing, and I've seen better days myself!'

The angel Gabriel announced the fact that this would happen *in its own time* and because Zacharias had doubted God's Word and not by faith received it, Gabriel struck him dumb so that he was mute and could not speak! Whoa!

ALIGN YOUR CONFESSION WITH THE PROMISE

God spoke to me about this passage of scripture because in many ways I felt like God had done the same to me. I felt *dumb* because I seemingly had no new language for the new season I was about to embark on, but at the same time I knew it was time to move. *I was dumbstruck with a promise!*

You see, until you get a new mind and a new attitude, you won't be able to transition effectively. Because if you bring the old man into the new season, he's going to tear up everything that God has ordained for you to have. So God needs you to transition in your thinking.

What Zacharias had to understand was that 'his son John' or 'the promise' that he and Elizabeth were about to conceive, would not be a repeat of history. This thing would be something completely new and it would be something they had never seen before. And until Zacharias lined up his philosophy and his way of thinking with God's, he would remain speechless and dumbstruck.

The name John is significant because it was an 'unfitting

name'. No one in Zacharias' or Elizabeth's bloodline had ever been called by that name before. It was a name that was *unattached* and *unconnected* to anyone they had previously known.

Again, God said to me, 'The promise that I am about to give you has never been seen by you before, therefore it will seem unfitting and unfamiliar.' God also said, 'It, too, will seem unfitting and unfamiliar to those around you but you cannot let this affect your decision to step out and move on.'

In Luke 1:59-64 we find that Zacharias' and Elizabeth's relatives marvelled or were shocked when they decided to call the child John. They were obviously thrown by the fact that this was something out of the box and disconnected; something for which they could find no reference point.

Again God whispered into my heart concerning my future, that, 'This next season will not be a repeat of the past, but it will be something new and fresh. Some will ask questions about your motives and intentions but you must not let them sway you.'

When the child John was being circumcised and dedicated to the Lord, we find that Zacharias was still unable to speak, he was still dumbstruck. However, when the time came to publicly name the child, Zacharias wrote down his name on a chalkboard. Immediately after he did this, his tongue became loosed!

I remember God saying to me, 'Mark, the moment you line up your life with the things I'm asking of you and by faith begin to walk them out, I will loose things into your life. I will loose the people, I will loose the provision and I will loose the promotion. Just be obedient.'

FAITH BY OBEDIENCE

As soon as I stepped out in faith and began to believe God at His Word, things started to move in my life. I discovered a life that had been *waiting for me!* A strategic meeting that I created caused me to meet some new people who then introduced me to other like-minded individuals who then, in turn, introduced me to others and, quickly, new doors began to open.

I began consulting and building into other local church ministries, I travelled and preached, I ministered and led worship. I began to think and create in a new way. It was wonderful partnering with God in a whole new fashion, watching Him one by one open up doors of opportunity for me. I hadn't seen anything like this for so long.

Now my transition didn't really look ordered. It actually felt like I was making it up as I went along. But what I learned was this: for a while I was going to have to get used to not being able to see clearly. But as I began to build new relationships and familiarise myself with the flow of a new way of thinking, I became more comfortable with it.

When a caterpillar is in the chrysalis, in the midst of its *metamorphosis* and has not yet become a butterfly, it can't see a thing, it's in the dark! But behind the scenes and hidden away from everyone else's view something magnificent is taking place, a whole new being is created, a butterfly is being born! So if you're in transition right now, be encouraged because the same is happening to you. Someone new is being created and will soon be born!

Transition can be a lonely place at times because you are not only letting go of what you used to do, but you're letting go of those you used to do it with. I have come to realise that a lot of the people that I thought were life-long relationships were not really that at all. We were relationally connected to the purpose of *'ministry'* but when that began to change so did our relationship. When I began to flow outside of the ministry and purpose we were connected to for a season, we stopped seeing each other. Now I'm not blaming anyone for that; that's just the way it is. So I learned that in my transition I was going to have to be strong on my own for a season and be strong in the realisation that I was going to have to forge new friendships and build new relationships.

The beautiful thing I discovered was there were people up ahead of me, attached to my future, that I had not yet been acquainted with who would be vital friendships for me. They unknowingly and some knowingly would help catapult me into the next stage of my journey. They would *think like me* and *sound like me*. We would understand each other's language and we would be able to connect on the same level of thought and experience. There were also other relationships that would glean from the things that I had learned in order for them to move into their next season. God releases us so that we can release others.

ALL GREAT CHANGES ARE PRECEDED BY CHAOS!

You know, friend, *change is inevitable*. God does not want you to stay the same. You can't experience all that He has for your life without change. You have to let go of something that you are familiar with to find something new. If you want to enjoy different scenery you've got to leave your hometown. But the reality is, change can be chaotic and change can be messy but that doesn't make it wrong. Actually, that's what makes it right most of the time.

There are so many factors that are affected during a time of transition that trying to tidy them up is almost impossible. People's lives are radically affected. Relationships change. Roles and duties shift. Families are uprooted as locations are changed. Unfortunately sometimes intentions are misread and misjudged, and the list goes on. So it is only natural that chaos will precede your locking into your next season. But if it's a God thing then you're in good hands! Everything will work itself out. It may take a while but eventually the dust will settle and you will be able to see the beauty of a new land and new terrain that God has ready for you to explore and enjoy!

I hope this last chapter has helped you and has given you some wisdom and tools that will help you if you're going through a season of transition. I have tried to be as transparent as possible so that you can effectively move on into all that God has called you to do. If you feel that God is stirring up your nest and making you feel uncomfortable where you are right now, then I believe it's most likely your time to *leap from the nest, spread out those wings and FLY!*

May God bless your every move, friend, and may God bless your every step as you transition into your glorious future!

PRAYER

I hope you enjoyed this book and that it has been both a blessing and a challenge to your life and walk with God. Maybe you just got hold of it and are looking through before starting. Long ago, I made the decision never to take for granted that everyone has prayed a prayer to receive Jesus as their Lord, so I am including that as the finale to this book. If you have never asked Jesus into your life and would like to do that now, it's so easy. Just pray this simple prayer:

> *Dear Lord Jesus, thank You for dying on the cross for me. I believe that You gave Your life so that I could have life. When You died on the cross, You died as an innocent man who had done nothing wrong. You were paying for my sins and the debt I could never pay. I believe in You, Jesus, and receive the brand new life and fresh start that the Bible promises that I can have. Thank You for my sins forgiven, for the righteousness that comes to me as a gift from You, for hope and love beyond what I have known and the assurance of eternal life that is now mine. Amen.*

Good next moves are to get yourself a Bible that is easy to

understand and begin to read. Maybe start in John so you can discover all about Jesus for yourself. Start to pray – prayer is simply talking to God – and, finally, find a church that's alive and get your life planted in it. These simple ingredients will cause your relationship with God to grow.

STRENGTH
FOR THE
ROAD

OTHER RESOURCES BY
MARK STEVENS

Keep up to date with Mark Stevens through his website and social media:

markstevensmusic.com

facebook.com/mark.stevensawe

twitter.com/marklstevens

instagram.com/marklstevens

OTHER RESOURCES BY MARK STEVENS

Mark's first solo album

To Be With You

Track Listing:
1. To Be With You
2. Red
3. Great Is The Lord
4. Underneath Your Wings
5. To Know Your Love
6. Nothing Can Tear Us Apart
7. Clearly Now
8. How Lovely You Are
9. Fight For Love (Live)
10. Monsoon Rain

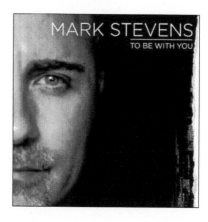

An album of eclectic and unique songs, inspired by Mark's testimony of transformation; songs that were birthed through an intimate and passionate relationship with his Saviour.

Available from iTunes, Amazon and markstevensmusic.com.

Mark's next album will be released late summer 2014.

FURTHER INFORMATION

For further information about the author of this book, or to order more copies, please contact:

Great Big Life Publishing
Empower Centre
83-87 Kingston Road
Portsmouth
Hants
PO2 7DX
UK

info@greatbiglifepublishing.com
www.greatbiglifepublishing.com
@GBLPublishing

ARE YOU AN AUTHOR?

Do you have a word from God on your heart that you're looking to get published to a wider audience? We're looking for manuscripts that identify with our own vision of bringing life-giving and relevant messages to the Body of Christ. Send yours for review towards possible publication to:

Great Big Life Publishing
Empower Centre
83-87 Kingston Road
Portsmouth
Hants
PO2 7DX
UK

or, email us at info@greatbiglifepublishing.com